RACIST, SEXIST, RUDE, CRUDE AND DISHONEST

The Golden Age of Madison Avenue

Booth-Clibborn Editions

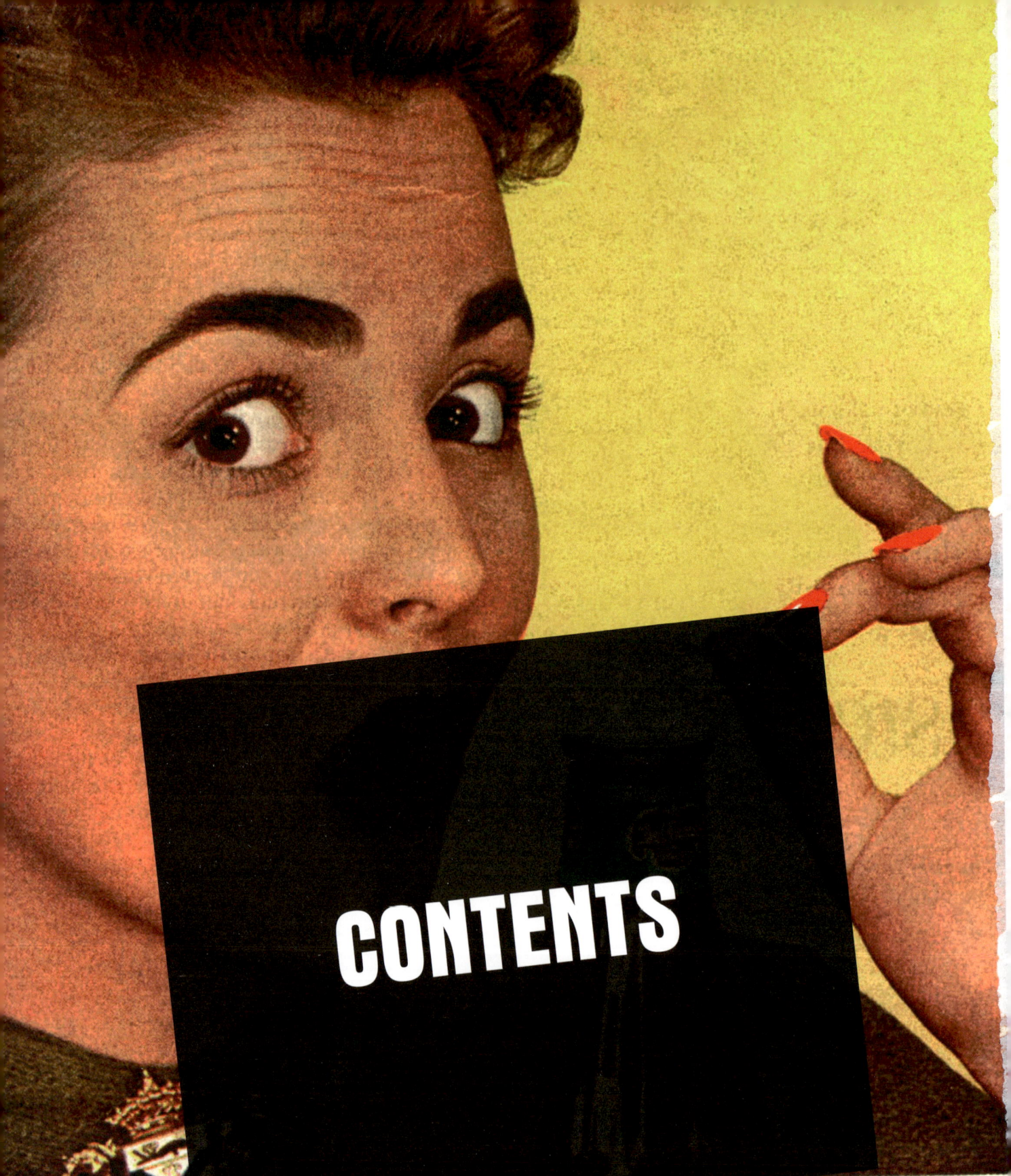

CONTENTS

mean a **woman** can open it

1

KEEP
HER
WHERE
SHE
BELONGS...

If your husband ever finds out

you're not "store-testing" for fresher coffee...

...if he discovers you're still taking chances on getting flat, stale coffee ...woe be unto you! For today there's a sure and certain way to test for freshness before you buy

Here's how easy it is to be sure of fresher coffee

Look for the "Dome Top" Can of Chase & Sanborn. That firm, rounded top shows it's packed *under pressure*, fresh from the oven.

Just do this:

Press your thumbs against the dome top *before* you buy. If it's firm, it's fresh. If the top clicks, pressure's gone—take another. It's the one way to get the freshest coffee ever packed.

No other can lets you test!

You can't test an ordinary flat top can. Some are "leakers" that have let air in to steal freshness. But all flat top cans look alike. You can't tell which are good and which are stale.

Here's the payoff!

Sure as you pour a cup, they'll want more! For Chase & Sanborn is a glorious blend of more expensive coffees . . . brought to you *fresher*. No wonder Chase & Sanborn pays a flavor dividend you won't find in any other coffee!

REGULAR GRIND
NEW NEW
PRESSURE PACKED
Chase & Sanborn
COFFEE

"PRESSURE PACKED"

Chase & Sanborn

Chase & Sanborn, Compton Advertising Agency, *Life*, 1952

Blow in her face and she'll follow
you anywhere...

In the middle of the last century,
marketing men had few qualms
about creating brutally sexist
advertisements.

Brushing off any criticism of being
misogynistic, they would dryly
explain that misogynists are men
who don't hate women as much as
women hate each other.

It was an age when few would grasp
the concept of political correctness.

This doesn't diminish the bewildering
bad manners of so much of the
advertising, offensive to the point
of callousness.

The simmering implication that ran through campaigns such as Chase & Sanborn coffee,[7] Mr Legg's slacks, and Van Heusen shirts is that a man should be on top, and he should maintain this dominance through physical intimidation.

Women were literally under a man's heel, or down at his feet, keen to have him 'walk all over her' – indeed in the Van Heusen shirt campaign a man spanking his wife is 'daring'.[14]

Women are to be tamed through a male's sheer magnetism – who can resist a man in a great pair of slacks, or his brute force?

It's nice to have a girl around the house.

Though she was a tiger lady, our hero didn't have to fire a shot to floor her. After one look at his **Mr. Leggs** slacks, she was ready to have him walk all over her. That noble styling sure soothes the savage heart! If you'd like your own doll-to-doll carpeting, hunt up a pair of these he-man **Mr. Leggs** slacks. Such as our new automatic wash-wear blend of 65% "**Dacron***" and 35% rayon—incomparably wrinkle-resistant. About **$12.95** at plush-carpeted stores.

Dacron ™ *for Fall!*

✧ Du Pont's Registered Trade Mark

Get yourself a new pair of **Mr. Leggs** ®

THOMSON COMPANY, 1290 Avenue of the Americas, New York 19, N. Y.

Mr Leggs, Henry Bach & Associates, Inc. Agency, *Esquire*, 1964

Keep her where she belongs...

with **WEYENBERG MASSAGIC**

Shoe illustrated sells for about $35.00—For name of your nearest dealer, write: Weyenberg Shoe Mfg. Co., Milwaukee, Wisc. 53201.

Weyenberg Massagic, *Playboy*, 1972

Tipalet cigars ran their 'Blow in her face and she'll follow you anywhere...' campaign in the 1960s.[17] The ad demonstrated a spectacular convergence of unpleasant marketing techniques – not to mention the product itself, a cigar with a tip flavoured with cherry and blueberry amongst other essences.

A wide eyed sixties 'babe', low cut top, open mouth and tanned skin, leans in to a dark handsome smoker who seductively blows smoke over her face. The phallic cigar acts as an extension of the man's sexual virility, and the woman is helplessly attracted.

The emphasis here is firmly on women as passive sexual objects manipulated by male powers of attraction.

The women's liberation movement, with the second wave of feminism being firmly and loudly underway at the time, didn't appear to cut much ice with marketing men.

This theme continues in the advertisement for the Cigar Institute of America.[15] A 'single girl' kneels in front of a suited cigar smoker holding aloft an ashtray. She recognises his masculine power and sophistication, and pays homage.

Cigar campaigns differ from their cigarette counterparts in that they address only men. The cigar smoker is depicted as highly superior, in turn cultivated and sexually dominant.

it's daring

it's audacious

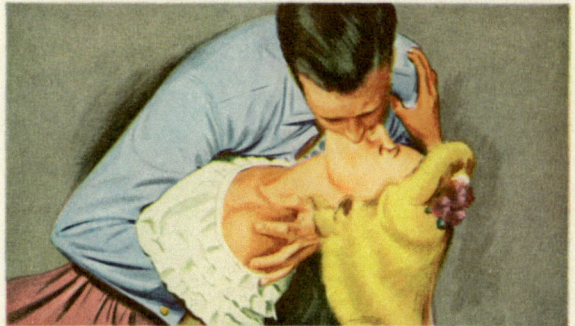

it's the **bolder look**

in

shirts

You never know what results you'll get until you try!
If you're the kind of a guy who shrinks from a violet or shies
from a sky blue shirt—just *try* one with your dark blue suit and
see what happens. For the Bold Look is an air, an
attitude, a spirit of bravado. It's reflected in clear bright colors
—11 of them and white. It's evident in the wide spread
collar, in the half-inch stitching, in the extra wide center pleat,
that distinguish this new Van Heusen shirt.
The quality's Van Heusen too: magic sewmanship;
laboratory-tested fabrics—*you get a new*
shirt free if your Van Heusen shrinks out of size!

The Van Bold Shirt, French or single cuffs, $3.95
The Bold Look Tie with Balloon Dots, $2

Phillips-Jones Corp., New York 1, N. Y.   Makers of
Van Heusen Shirts • Ties • Pajamas • Collars • Sport Shirts

Van Heusen shirts
REG. U. S. PAT. OFF.
the world's smartest

White   Peach   Lavender   Chartreuse   Rosewine   Sky Blue   Sunset Pink   Ecorn   Mist Grey   Sand Tan   Straw Yellow   Sage Green

Van Heusen, *Life*, 1949

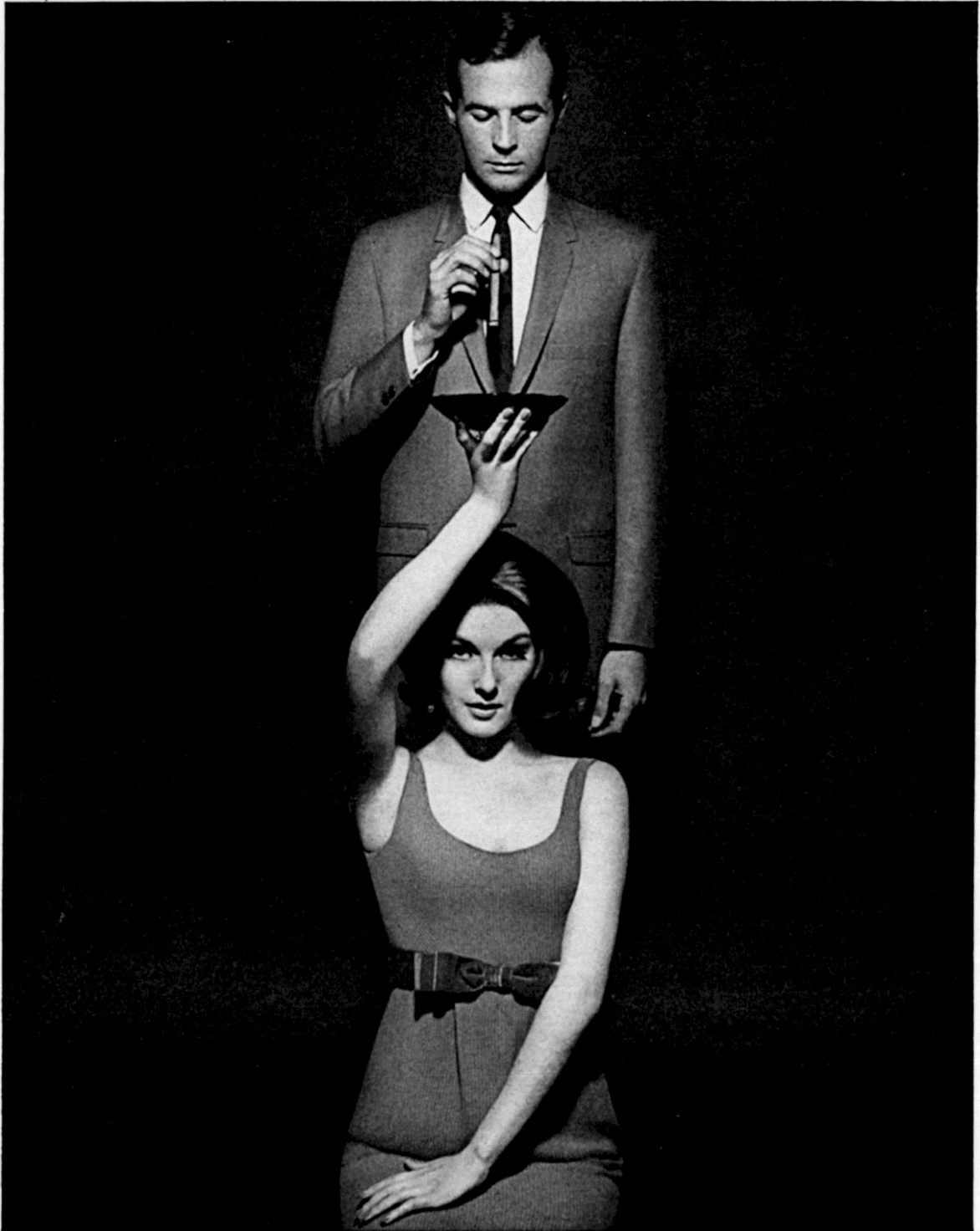

Suit by EAGLE CLOTHES/Dress by RUTH WALTER, Inc.

Why are more single girls switching to cigar smokers?

Chances are she saw him before he saw her. She knows he'll treat her as he would a cigar: tenderly, affectionately, appreciatively. What's more, cigar smokers start young and stay young ... very important for girls with long range plans. *and everyone knows you need not inhale to enjoy the rich flavor.*

CIGAR INSTITUTE OF AMERICA, INC.

Cigar Institute of America, David J. Mendelsohn Agency, 1962

Blunter still are the depictions of female weakness and inferiority used in adverts for Weyenberg shoes[14] and Warner's.

The latter celebrates new 'springlets' in a girdle, leaving behind the bone-reinforced corsetry that had pained women for decades.[18]

Whilst the evolution of women's undergarments was itself a story of liberation – ending in the bra burnings of the women's liberation movement – here the comfort a woman can have in her underwear is somewhat undermined by the image of her being cheerfully dragged by her hair by her 'bone-age' husband.

Blow in her face and she'll follow you anywhere.

Hit her with tangy Tipalet Cherry. Or rich, grape-y Tipalet
Burgundy. Or luscious Tipalet Blueberry. It's Wild!
Tipalet. It's new. Different. Delicious in taste and in aroma.
A puff in her direction and she'll follow you, anywhere.
Oh yes... you get smoking satisfaction without inhaling smoke.

Smokers of America,
do yourself a flavor.
Make your next
cigarette a

Tipalet.®

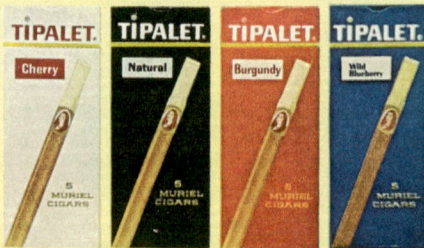

New from Muriel.   About 5 for 25¢.

Tipalet, Young & Rubicam Agency, *Playboy*, 1970

#952-953, with strong leno elastic sides, a down-stretching satin elastic back. White, $16.50. The bra—#1045 at $3.95

Come out of the bone age, darling…

Warner's exclusive new STA-FLAT replaces pokey bones with circular springlets

Progress…it's wonderful! Warner's takes the cave-man manners out of old-fashioned girdles (poke, shove, groan), removes those long front bones that dug into your midriff. Now control's achieved with light springlets pocketed in the girdle's front panel. They're light and flexible — modern as your way of life, sensible as vitamins.

Far better control, too—STA-FLAT

gives not just pinpoint support, like old-fashioned bones, but firms a greater area with lively comfort. Bend, breathe, sit … STA-FLAT† moves through the day with you, responds to every movement of your body…all with unbelievable lightness, and giving you extra support where you need it most (midriff, waist, tummy).

You don't need to wear armor to be a

charmer. Warner's is happy to give the dinosaur his due — but not on *you*. Come out, beautifully, into the light, free whirl of today! You'll find it at your nicest store.

WARNER'S*

* REG. U. S. PAT. OFF. † TRADE MARK

Bras • Girdles • Corselettes

Warner's, Doyle Dane Bernbach Agency, *New Yorker*, 1955

Give her a Hoover and you give her the best

Christmas morning
(and forever after)
she'll be happier
with a Hoover

P.S. to husbands:
She cares about her home, you know, so if you really care about her
. . . wouldn't it be good to consider a Hoover for Christmas?
Prices start at $66.95. Model 29 (shown here) $95.95. Low down
payment; easy terms. See your Hoover dealer now.

THE HOOVER COMPANY
North Canton, Ohio

Hoover, Erwin Wasey Agency, 1951

The harder she works...

The feminine psyche was under assault on all fronts; she must take into consideration beauty, weight, eternal youth, both attractive enough to keep her man, and the ideal housewife and mother.

A Kellogg's advert shows the key attributes that define a wife – small waisted, hard working, perfect hair, and that all-important ready smile for the returning husband.

What marked a departure was the engineering of food. Kellogg's PEP was a new brand of cereal that was infused with vitamins – a blend that ensured the happy wife would keep up with the housework.[24]

The housewife, instituted by magazines, advertising and films, was a figure targeted steadily by marketeers eagerly selling the newest frontier in comsumerables – domestic appliances.

The Hotpoint ad overleaf implores the male reader, i.e. the one with the chequebook, to 'Please…let your wife come into the living room'.[26] A slender wife washes infinite dishes whilst the rest of the family happily bonds in front of the TV next door.

Dishwashers, along with Hoovers, freezers and other household appliances, were part of the post-war boom, when it seemed your patriotic duty to consume.

The dishwasher was in fact the invention of a woman – Josephine Cochrane, who exhibited her version at the 1893 Chicago World's Fair. A very wealthy lady, her main household gripe would be that her servants couldn't wash-up fast enough and were always chipping her fine china.

Essentially, advertisers were actively enlisted by the government to push women back into housewifely roles after the war had introduced millions to the world of work.

Many wanted to remain in their jobs, enjoying the wages and independence that was afforded them, but the government felt that returning war vets needed the support of the family structure, and American society needed the security of gendered roles.

Vitamins for pep! **PEP** for vitamins!*

Kellogg's, N.W Ayer & Son Agency, 1938

Please...let your wife

● **Doing dishes** the Hotpoint workless way is easy and costs only a few pennies a day. You simply put the dishes in the Hotpoint Automatic Dishwasher, turn one switch and the job's done. Everything—dishes, silverware, pots, pans and casseroles—is double-washed, double-rinsed and dried electrically.

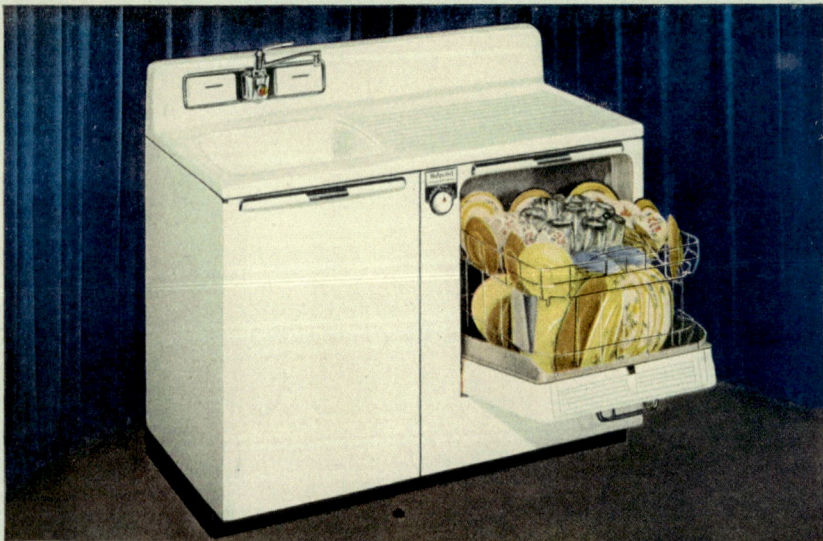

Guaranteed by
Good Housekeeping

LOOK TO HOTPOINT FOR THE FINEST — FIRST!

RANGES • REFRIGERATORS

Hotpoint, Batten, Barton, Durstine & Osborn Agency, *Life*, 1950

come into the living room!

DON'T let dirty dishes make your wife a kitchen exile! She loses the most precious hours of her life shut off from pleasures of the family circle by the never-ending chore of old-fashioned dishwashing! Please . . . let her come into the living room. It's easy to banish the barrier of dishpan drudgery so she can join the family fun—the modern, automatic Hotpoint way!

● **The wonderful,** new Hotpoint Automatic Electric Dishwasher is the greatest time- and labor-saving appliance ever invented for the home. It also protects your family's health by doing dishes the sanitary way—many, many times cleaner than is possible by hand. And it saves your wife at least an extra hour every day—seven hours a week—that she can devote to happier home-making for the entire family! Hotpoint Inc. (*A General Electric Affiliate*), 5600 West Taylor Street, Chicago 44, Illinois.

Everybody's Pointing To

Hotpoint

Automatic ● Electric Dishwashers

But in fact by 1960 twice as many women were in work than had been in 1940, and 40% of women over sixteen had a job – albeit jobs deemed 'womanly' or too lowly for men.

However, this revolution, spurred by women's wartime experience, would soon serve to undermine the image of housewifery projected by advertisers.

A rosy cheeked housewife is amazed that she can actually manage to open a ketchup bottle 'without a husband'! The Alcoa Hytop bottle cap was aimed at being considerate of the feebleness of womankind, touching on the technological advances in the post-war environment, when industry was redirected from the war effort to focus on fuelling consumption.

Adland had apparently forgotten that women were perfectly capable of building tanks, bombs, and machine guns in America's munitions factories between 1941 and 1945.

And today, I wonder how many women would be charmed by a husband's Christmas gift of a new Hoover.[21]

You mean a <u>woman</u> can open it ?

Easily—without a knife blade, a bottle opener, or even a husband! All it takes is a dainty grasp, an easy, two-finger twist—and the catsup is ready to pour.

We call this safe-sealing bottle cap the Alcoa HyTop. It is made of pure, food-loving Alcoa Aluminum. It spins off—and back on again—without muscle power because an exclusive Alcoa process tailors it to each bottle's threads after it is on the bottle. By vacuum sealing both top and sides, the HyTop gives purity a double guard.

You'll recognize the attractive, tractable HyTop when you see it on your grocer's shelf. It's long, it's white, it's grooved—and it's on the most famous and flavorful brands. Put the bottle that wears it in your basket . . . save fumbling, fuming and fingers at opening time with the most cooperative cap in the world—the Alcoa HyTop Closure.

Alcoa Aluminum

Alcoa Aluminium, Fuller & Smith & Ross, Inc. Agency, 1953

Would your husband marry you again?

FORTUNATE is the woman who can answer "yes." But many a woman, if she is honest with herself, is forced to be in doubt—after that she pays stricter attention to her personal attractions.

A radiant skin, glowing and healthy, is more than a "sign" of youth. It *is* youth. And any woman can enjoy it.

Beauty's basis

is pure, mild, soothing soap. Never go to sleep without using it. Women should never overlook this all-important fact. The basis of beauty

Volume and efficiency enable us to sell Palmolive for

10c

is a thoroughly clean skin. And the only way to it is soap.

There is no harm in cosmetics, or in powder or rouge, if you frequently remove them. Never leave them on overnight.

The skin contains countless glands and pores. These clog with oil, with dirt, with perspiration—with refuse from within and without.

The first requirement is to cleanse those pores. And soap alone can do that.

A costly mistake

Harsh, irritating soaps have led many women to omit soap. That is a costly mistake. A healthy, rosy, clear, smooth skin is a clean skin, first of all. There is no need for using a soap which irritates. Palmolive soothes and softens while it cleans. It contains palm and olive oils.

Force the lather into the pores by a gentle massage. Every touch is balmy. Then all the foreign matter comes out in the rinsing.

If your skin is very dry, use cold cream before and after washing.

No medicaments

Palmolive is just a soothing, cleansing soap. Its blandness comes through blending palm and olive oils. Nothing since the world began has proved so suitable for delicate complexions.

All its beneficial effects come through gentle, thorough cleaning. There are no medicaments. No drugs can do what Nature does when you aid her with this scientific Palmolive cleansing.

Millions of women get their envied complexions through the use of Palmolive soap.

The Palmolive Company, Milwaukee, U. S. A. The Palmolive Company of Canada, Limited, Toronto, Ont.

Palm and olive oils were royal cosmetics in the days of ancient Egypt

Copyright 1921, The Palmolive Co. 1241

Brett Litho. Co., N.

More searching than your mirror...

The name of the man or woman who coined the phrase 'sex sells' is lost in time.

This truism is core to the history of advertising, and in the first half of the twentieth century sexual politics dominated much of marketing. Watching its pathways you discern changing attitudes to gender – with the marketing voice being a conservative and generally depressing one for women.

The development of psychology led advertisers to a nearer understanding of the deep desires of men and women, the flows of the unconscious mind, and how choices between products are made and could be affected.

The desire to attract a partner, to fall in love and to keep that love fresh was an aspect of female and male behaviour that would come to be neatly manipulated.

Rather than just telling women that this or that product would keep them young, marketeers in campaigns like Palmolive preyed on the fear of losing a partner as a way to encourage women to use their soap as part of a simple beauty routine. Tantalising illustrations of soft skin, rosebud mouths and silk garments populated this campaign.

Admakers were also finding it far easier to reach women. Tabloid newspapers, celebrity and confession magazines were achieving soaring circulation numbers.

"More searching than your mirror ... your husband's eyes"

Over 20,000 beauty experts for that reason insist that clients keep skin radiantly young by using an olive and palm oil soap. Palmolive is the only large-selling soap made of these oils.

"IF ALL the women who seek to hold their husbands would first hold their good looks, editors of beauty columns wouldn't get such a large mail ... and there would be greater chances for happiness." That's the warning addressed to women by leading beauty specialists.

* * *

Neither a great amount of time nor large sums of money are necessary to keep looking your best. But intelligent home care, every day, *is* necessary. Don't think that means hours of primping. It means the best natural skin cleansing you can obtain. And beauty experts are unanimous in their recommendation of Palmolive facial cleansing.

Two minutes. That's all it takes. A simple washing of face and throat with the lather of this olive and palm oils soap. Then, powder, rouge, if you wish. But foundation cleansing, first.

Won't you try this method, endorsed by more than 20,000 experts, as the wisest step toward keeping that schoolgirl complexion? Use Palmolive ... twice every day ... faithfully. Then see what your mirror reveals. See what your husband's eyes reveal.

Retail Price
10c

"When you are in doubt as to the claims a soap makes, look at the label. Can you tell what's in that soap? Then why take chances? Use Palmolive—which is recommended by those who KNOW."
Carsten, Berlin's Distinguished Beauty Expert.

Keep that Schoolgirl Complexion

Palmolive, Lord & Thomas Agency, *Photoplay*, 1924

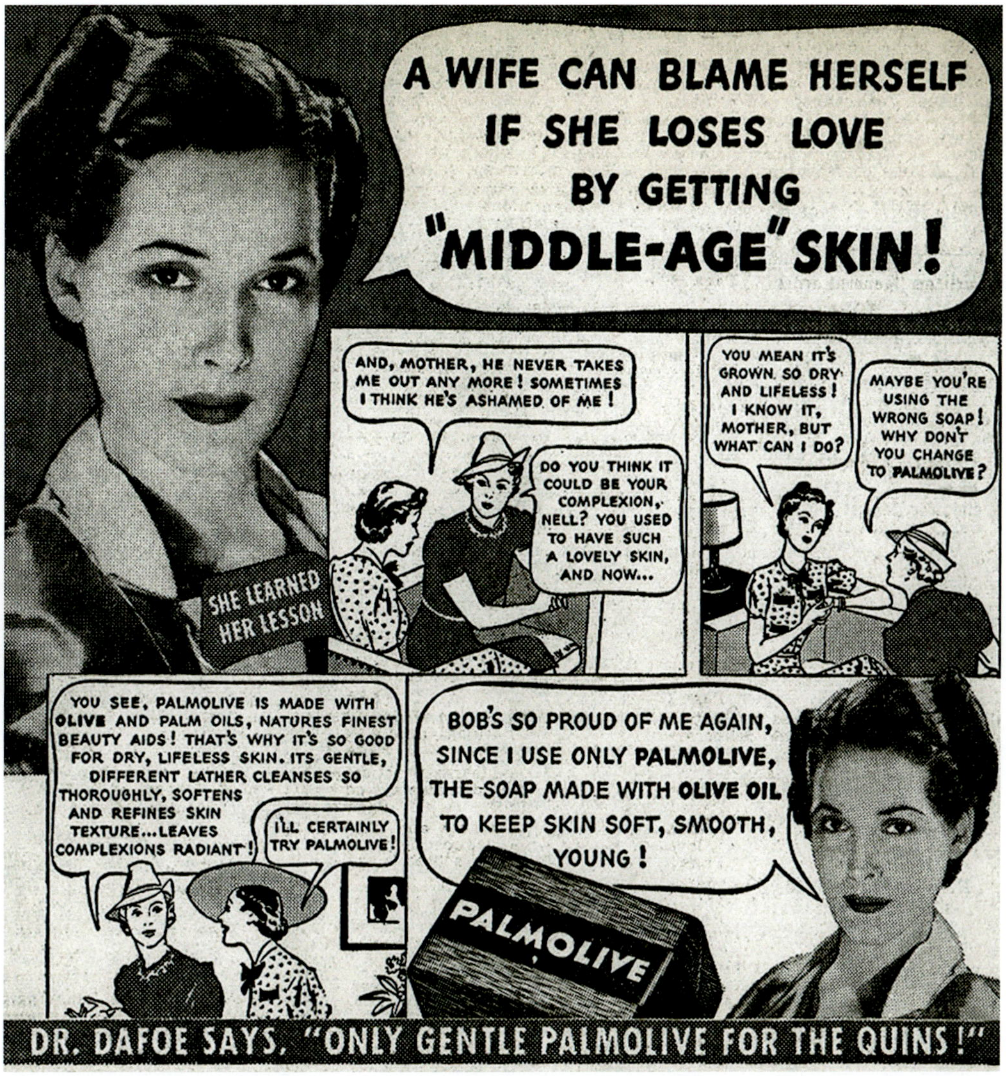

Palmolive, Benton & Bowles Agency, 1938

Gray Hair Cost Her Her Job!

She was willing and capable, but gray hair made her look old and slow. "A younger woman would work more snappily," was the verdict.

Gray hair *does* make a person look old, but gray hair is an unnecessary burden. Today, many women—and men—know that a mixture of sage tea and sulphur actually restores gray, faded or streaked hair to its original life and color. You can either prepare the mixture at home yourself, or more conveniently, buy it already prepared and ready to use. All druggists carry it in the form of Wyeth's Sage & Sulphur, and since the cost is only 75c a bottle, there is really no need to prepare it yourself. You simply moisten a comb or soft brush with it and draw it through your hair, one strand at a time. One application banishes the gray and one or two more completely restore your hair to its original color, so evenly, so naturally that no one can possibly tell you have used it.

The latter focused on first-person stories of romances and tragic heartbreaks and were aimed at young working women. Advertisers realised that they could now speak to working class, poor and black women who had previously been ignored as a market.

By 1930 money spent on toiletries was ten times higher than 20 years earlier. Where a women used to buy only a face powder, her cosmetic reptoire would now include dozens of make-up and skincare items.

Much soap advertising reinforced a message that it's a woman's prerogative to be a sexual object in the home.

All women should share the desire
to remain magically young – the
only state of womanhood that a man
could possibly wish for – and to be
the object of male attention.

The Palmolive campaign plays on
the mythic conception of romantic
love, staging their advertisements
in a constant twilight of silk dresses
and cocktails.[31] What is the use of
intelligence when your husband will
leave you because you look aged?

You are in a
BEAUTY CONTEST
every hour
of every day!

A CAKE of Camay Soap—and you have the finest beauty treatment in the world. Buy a dozen cakes—today—and watch this gentle soap bring out the natural beauty of your skin. With Camay your skin will glow with new, deep cleanliness!

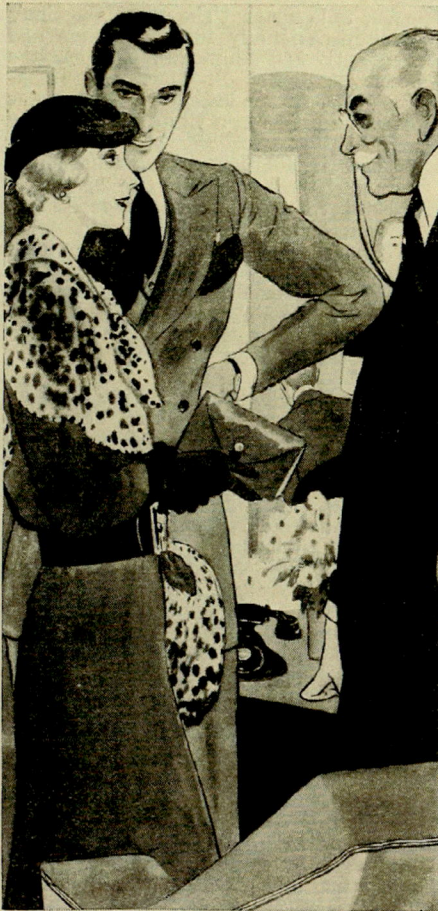

Natural loveliness begins with immaculate cleanliness. But be sure you use only the most delicate, the safest, of beauty soaps on your precious skin!

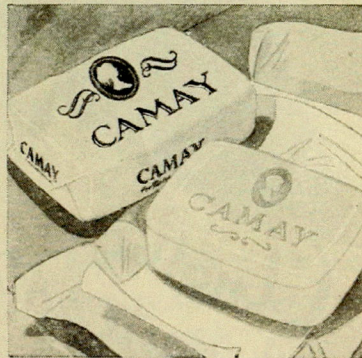

The girl above is meeting her husband's big chief! What impression would you make if you were in her Beauty Contest? Every man, from office boy to president, responds to clean, natural loveliness.

Delicate Camay, the Soap of Beautiful Women. Resolve to begin its use today and open up a new era of beauty for yourself and your precious skin!

CAMAY

Copr. 1932, Procter & Gamble Co.

THE SOAP OF BEAUTIFUL WOMEN

Love's Baby Soft.
Because innocence is sexier than you think.

Love's Baby Soft® is that irresistible, clean-baby smell, grown-up enough to be sexy. It's soft-smelling. Pure and innocent. It may well be the sexiest fragrance around.

Love Cosmetics

Love Cosmetics, Wells, Rich, Greene Agency, 1975

Procurable women...

For centuries women have had to
deal with the dichotomy of being
cast as angel or whore. Nowhere
is this better demonstrated than
through the medium of advertising.

We've seen women as housewives;
pretty, useful, hardworking, loving.
And we've seen them as whores
when it comes to an irresistible man
in slacks blowing cigar smoke. The
lengths to which advertisers have
used sexualised images of women to
appeal to buyers is mystifying, given
that this eroticism is often aimed at
women themselves as the target
audience for the product.

When Love Cosmetics was launched
it claimed 'Love's baby soft. Because
innocence is sexier than you think'
– alongside the image of a pre-
pubescent girl with a teddy bear.[43]
Aimed at young girls coming into
womanhood, this was the smell of
the ideal teen prom queen.

Griffin Microshine featured scantily
clothed women to purvey their brand
of boot and shoe shine. A woman's
breasts are prominently displayed
as she laughingly bowls at an alley,
a weak pun linking the two 'you'll
bowl them over with...'

In another, a near-naked women
sits at the bottom of the chimney
admiring the shine on Father
Christmas's boots. Broomsticks
Slacks walked a fine line in many
of their advertisements.[47] Gang rape?
Sexual assault? Just make sure to
do it in a pair of Broomsticks
because their Acrilan will never
lose its crease.

Right down the Alley—
with a Microsheen Shine!

You'll really bowl 'em over whenever
you sport a MICROSHEEN shine.
That's because MICROSHEEN is right
down the alley when it comes to
keeping shoes at their sparkling best.
Costlier waxes, rare conditioning oils,
wonder-working silicones to impart
a long-lasting brilliance under
all weather conditions. Buy a can of
GRIFFIN MICROSHEEN today.
It's a "ten strike" every time!

GRIFFIN
MICROSHEEN
STAIN BOOT POLISH

GRIFFIN MICROSHEEN
STAIN BOOT POLISH
Black • Brown • Tan • Oxblood • Red
Cordovan • Mahogany • Blue • Neutral

NOW! FREE SHINE CLOTH IN EACH MICROSHEEN BOX—STILL ONLY 25¢

Griffin Microsheen, Geyer Agency, *Playboy*, 1957

Broomsticks, *GQ*, 1967

The copy runs 'The Game is
Broomsticks. Ring around Rosie.
Or Carol. Or Eleanor.' Inter-
changeable bikini clad women,
the requisite for every game. For
Lucky Tiger Hair Wax, Linda, Lola
and Louise have been shot, stuffed
and mounted to decorate the Lucky
Tiger's lair.[54]

Sexually available women were
apparently a genuine health threat
to American GIs during the wars.
In World War I, 18,000 service men
were taken out of action every
day due to sexually transmitted
diseases. By World War II
advertising men were enlisted
to help spread information about
avoiding these afflictions.

Of course, in these campaigns the blame for the spread of such diseases was laid squarely at the doors of women, and in 1941 the May Act was introduced to prevent women soliciting from within a certain radius of military bases, resulting in many arrests.

The figure of 'procurable' women with venereal diseases was put at 98% – a grand total that even the most devoted propagandist would have difficulty in explaining to his mother.

no matter how strenuous the action...

HARRIS DACRON® SLACKS ARE PRESSED FOR LIFE!

HARRIS®* SLACKS

Yes, the ⬛ (Pressed for Life) finish on your Harris Slacks will keep them neat and natural at all times . . . no matter how strenuous the "action" . . . The easy-care fabric, of course, is 65% **DACRON**® polyester and 35% combed cotton, a power-packed combination for durability and good looks. Popularly priced from 7.00 - 10.00 at leading men's and boys' stores.

HARRIS SLACKS, 110 W. 11TH ST., LOS ANGELES, CALIF.

*®Reg. Union Mfg. Co.   ®Du Pont's Reg. T.M.

Harris Slacks, *GQ*, 1967

On Lucky Tiger's current web
homepage it describes itself as
a 'barbershop classic'.

It explains that it has helped men
'get lucky' since 1935, and that every
man needs an edge in the hunt for
a lady. 'Become a ladies' man with
the Lucky Tiger range, as tools of the
trade for a master of seduction.'

Their moisturising shower cream
comes in a pack labelled 'Suds
for Studs'.

LINDA

LOLA

LOUISE

Lucky Tiger gets the gals!
(which one do you want) *

Gals just naturally go for guys who use Lucky Tiger! The lovelies love you with that Lucky Ti-groomed look. It keeps your hair he-man handsome ... naturally good looking, without "patent leather" shine.

Lucky Tiger covers your scalp and hair in *only 9 seconds!* Contains a new grooming agent which keeps your hair perfectly groomed but is not oily or greasy. Start using it now and look your best always!

BUTCH HAIR WAX Created by Lucky Tiger for the crew cuts. Holds hair up where it should be up—down where it should be down!

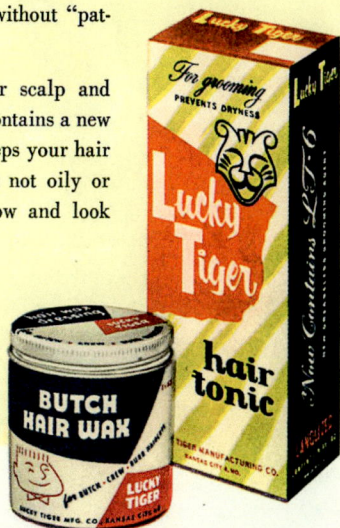

*Make Your Den a Lucky Lair
Send in a box-top from Lucky Tiger Hair Tonic or a label from Lucky Tiger "Butch" Hair Wax, and we'll send you a picture of Linda, Lola and Louise suitable for framing. *Mail to:*
LUCKY TIGER • 2901 FAIRMOUNT • KANSAS CITY 8, MISSOURI

ESQUIRE : *September*

Lucky Tiger, McCann Erickson Agency, *Esquire,* 1957

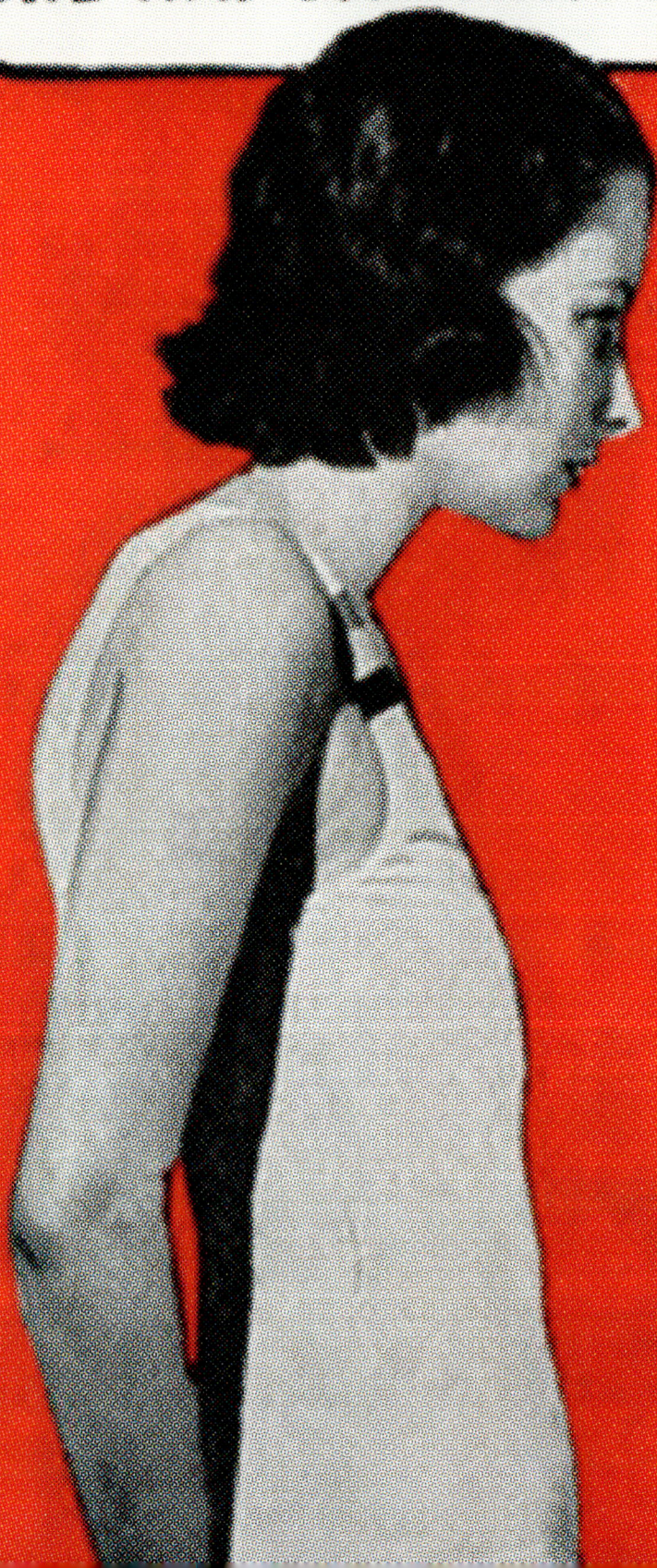

Add 5lbs of solid flesh in a week...

The notion of preying on a woman's lack of 'sex appeal' became an essential marketing tool in the 1930s and 40s for products aimed at fattening you up.

Advertisements declaring 'Skinny girls are not glamour girls', 'Skinny and lonely!', 'Men wouldn't look at me when I was skinny' were accompanied by beaming, full-figured, swimsuit-clad models to drive home the message that buxom is beautiful – to men at least.

Ironized Yeast and their competitors Kelp-a-Malt and Wate-On claimed to help 'beanpoles', who could now pile on the pounds with an ambiguous combination of 'essential elements' and 'food iodine'.

They were seen as 'remedies'
to alleviate the side effects of iron
deficiency, namely 'skinniness',
or as marketers chose to put it,
'scrawniness'.

Ironized Yeast called upon unnamed
scientists to proclaim that people
are thin and rundown only because
they don't get enough vitamin B and
iron from their daily food, resulting
in a lack of appetite and fatigue.

Kelp-a-Malt boasted that each tablet
contained more iron and copper
than 1lb of spinach, more calcium
than 3 eggs, more phosphorous than
1½ lbs of carrots, and more food
iodine than 1,600lbs of beef.

Some advertisers decided on giving
the skinny ailment a name – 'the gray
sickness'. Doctors today would call
the more extreme symptoms anaemia.

The gray sickness not only made you
thin, wan and miserable but also
contributed to premature aging,
due to your body drawing on
essential calcium and fat reserves
to make up for breaking the taboo
of being too thin.

GIRLS WITH "NATURALLY *Skinny* " FIGURES

...AMAZED AT THIS ENTIRELY NEW WAY TO ADD 5 LBS. OF SOLID FLESH IN 1 WEEK...OR NO COST!

New Natural Mineral Concentrate From the Sea, Rich in FOOD IODINE, Building Up Weak, Rundown Men and Women Everywhere.

THOUSANDS of thin, pale, rundown folks—and even "Naturally Skinny" men and women—are amazed at this new, easy way to put on healthy needed pounds quickly. Gains of 15 to 20 lbs. in one month—5 lbs. in one week—are reported regularly.

Kelp-a-Malt, the new mineral concentrate from the sea—gets right down to the cause of thin, underweight conditions and adds weight through a "3 ways in one" natural process.

First, its rich supply of easily assimilable minerals nourish the digestive glands, which produce the juices that alone enable you to digest the fats and starches, the weight-making elements in your daily diet. Second, Kelp-a-Malt provides an

amazingly effective digestive substance which actually digests 4 times its own weight of the flesh-building foods you eat. Third, Kelp-a-Malt's natural FOOD IODINE stimulates and nourishes the internal glands which control assimilation—the process of converting digested food into firm flesh, new strength and energy. Three Kelp-a-Malt tablets contain more iron and copper than a pound of spinach or $7\frac{1}{2}$ lbs. of fresh tomatoes; more calcium than 6 eggs; more phosphorous than $1\frac{1}{2}$ lbs. carrots; more FOOD IODINE than 1600 lbs. of beef.

Try Kelp-a-Malt for a single week and

Gained 15 lbs. on 1st bottle
"I gained 15 pounds on my first bottle of Kelp-a-Malt and noticed an improvement in strength, energy and vitality. Kelp-a-Malt's minerals were just what I needed."—Bill Riesen, Ashland, Mont.

notice the difference—how much better you sleep, how firm flesh appears in place of scrawny hollows and the new energy and strength it brings you! Prescribed and used by physicians, Kelp-a-Malt is fine for children, too — improves their appetites. Remember the name, Kelp-a-Malt, the original and genuine kelp and malt tablets. There is nothing else like them, so don't accept imitations and substitutes. Try Kelp-a-Malt today, and if you don't gain at least 5 lbs. of good, firm flesh in 1 week, the trial is free. 100 jumbo size tablets, 4 to 5 times the size of ordinary tablets, cost but little. Sold at all good drug stores. If your dealer has not yet received his supply, send $1.00 for special introductory size bottle of 65 tablets to address below.

KELP·A·MALT *Tablets*

SPECIAL FREE OFFER
Write today for fascinating instructive 50-page book on How to Add Weight Quickly. Mineral Contents of Food and their effects on the human body. New facts about FOOD IODINE. Standard weight and measurement charts. Daily menus for weight building. Absolutely free. No obligation. Kelp-a-Malt Co., Dept. 258, 27-33 West 20th St., New York City.

Whilst there are few convincing
case-studies to prove whether or not
these tablets worked (other than the
before and after pictures, which
were routinely two different women)
yeast does in fact aid weight gain,
and B vitamins do increase appetite.

And the reason for this pandemic
aversion to scrawniness?

Anxiety lingered after the Great
Depression that skinny bodies were
the result of people simply not
having enough to eat.

Ironized Yeast was seen as a quick
fix to health, and a disguise of near-
starvation.

In times of hardship mankind finds
inventive new ways to feed
themselves; during the Depression
families would eat whatever was to
hand; rabbits in the country and
squirrels in the city.

Women were taught to stretch their
food budgets by bulking meals with
potatoes and flour, and some less
than appetising delicacies also grew
in favour.

Fried potato peel sandwiches,
chicken feet in broth, cornmeal
mush, gravy and bread, oatmeal
mixed with lard, hand-picked

dandelion salad and even road kill became staples of questionable nutritional value.

Eventually, as prosperity grew in the following decades, eating for vanity rather than health became important.

A fuller figure became less desirable, and women chose to control their bodies through low calorie diets; the 800 calorie per day grapefruit and cabbage soup diets became popular, and continue to be used by dieters in search quick results today.

Hollywood stars such as Bette Davis paved the way for an enviable hourglass figure, waists shrunk down to as miniscule as 18 inches, some naturally and some through waist training corsets.

Girdles, which had been collecting dust at the back of wardrobes, were back in favour.

Using exercise to hone your body was developing; meanwhile, women were drawn to beauty treatments that entailed being pummeled and jiggled by large vibrating rollers.

These were thought to tighten up wobbly-bits without real physical exertion.

Avoiding the chore of exercise, well-to-do women went to extreme lengths to achieve the perfect figure.

HOW DO YOU LOOK IN YOUR BATHING SUIT

SKINNY ? THOUSANDS GAIN 10 TO 25 POUNDS THIS QUICK EASY WAY

Read how thin, tired-out, nervous, rundown peopl. have gained health and strength—*quick!*

ARE you ashamed to be seen in a bathing suit, because you're too skinny and scrawny-looking? Are you often tired, nervous—unable to eat and sleep properly?

Then here's wonderful news! Thousands of skinny, rundown men and women have gained 10 to 25 pounds and new pep — the women naturally alluring curves and new popularity—with this scientific vitamin-rich formula, Ironized Yeast.

Why it builds up so quick

Scientists have discovered that countless people are thin and rundown — tired, cranky, washed-out — only because they don't get enough Vitamin B and iron from their daily food. Without enough of these vital substances

you may lack appetite and not get the most body-building good out of what you eat.

Now you get these exact missing substances in these marvelous little Ironized Yeast tablets. No wonder, then, that they have helped thousands of people who n stances to gain new natu pounds, new health and pep and success—*often in just a fe*

Try them without ri:

Get Ironized Yeast tablets gist today. If with the fi don't eat better and FEEL b

Gains 11 lbs. New Pep. Now Has All The Dates She Wants

"When you're skinny, pale and sickly-looking, the fellows hardly look at you. I tried everything, but no good until I got Ironized Yeast. Soon I felt a lot peppier. In 4 weeks I gained 11 pounds. Now I have all the dates I want."

Ella Craig

Ella Craig, Lancaster, S. C.

No Longer a $ crow. Gains 14

"It's no fun to ha ing at you and ca I was so skinny out. Finally, I YEAST. In five w Now I go out good times."

Irvin Echard

Irvin Ec

Sylvia Ullbeck, otherwise known as Madame Sylvia, was a Hollywood legend, famous for sculpting the bodies of some of the most celebrated actresses of cinema's Golden Age.

Madame Sylvia was a trained masseuse who kept stars camera-ready by enforcing severe calorie counting along with massages so forceful that, as she revealed, the 'fat comes through the pores like mashed potato through a colander'.

Sylvia's general diet rules included never eating eggs older than 24 hours, having fruit only for a treat, plain pasta with butter, and never, under any circumstance, should you have any condiments or sauces with your meals.

Madame Sylvia fell from grace after publishing her clients' secrets in her book *Hollywood Undressed: Observations of Sylvia As Noted by Her Secretary*, and she then turned to writing for the first celebrity-gossip magazine *Photoplay*, sharing health tips with the public.

Of course, in more recent years the ideal body type for women would be promoted as very slender.

Advertising weight-gain is unheard of today, and the only similar products today are protein shakes aimed at men wanting to build muscle.

But even now dietary supplements
are still not regulated as stringently
as actual foods and medicines.

Manufacturers do not need to
register their products or obtain
approval before selling them, and it
continues to be disputed that taking
meal replacement supplements
makes any positive impact on your
health whatsoever.

With millions of people globally
struggling with obesity, it is
becoming harder for the majority
to achieve our skinny ideal, and the
US diet industry is currently worth
$60.9 billion.

The ultimate irony for women today
is that the malnourished 'before'
bodies, presented as so hopelessly
unappealing in the mid-twentieth
century, have become the
contemporary world's pinnacle
of desirability.

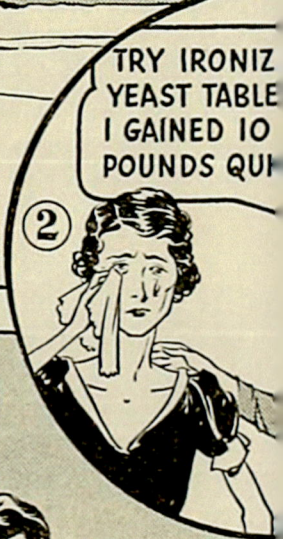

Ironized Yeast, Ruthrauff and Ryan Agency, *Radio Mirror*, 1937

79

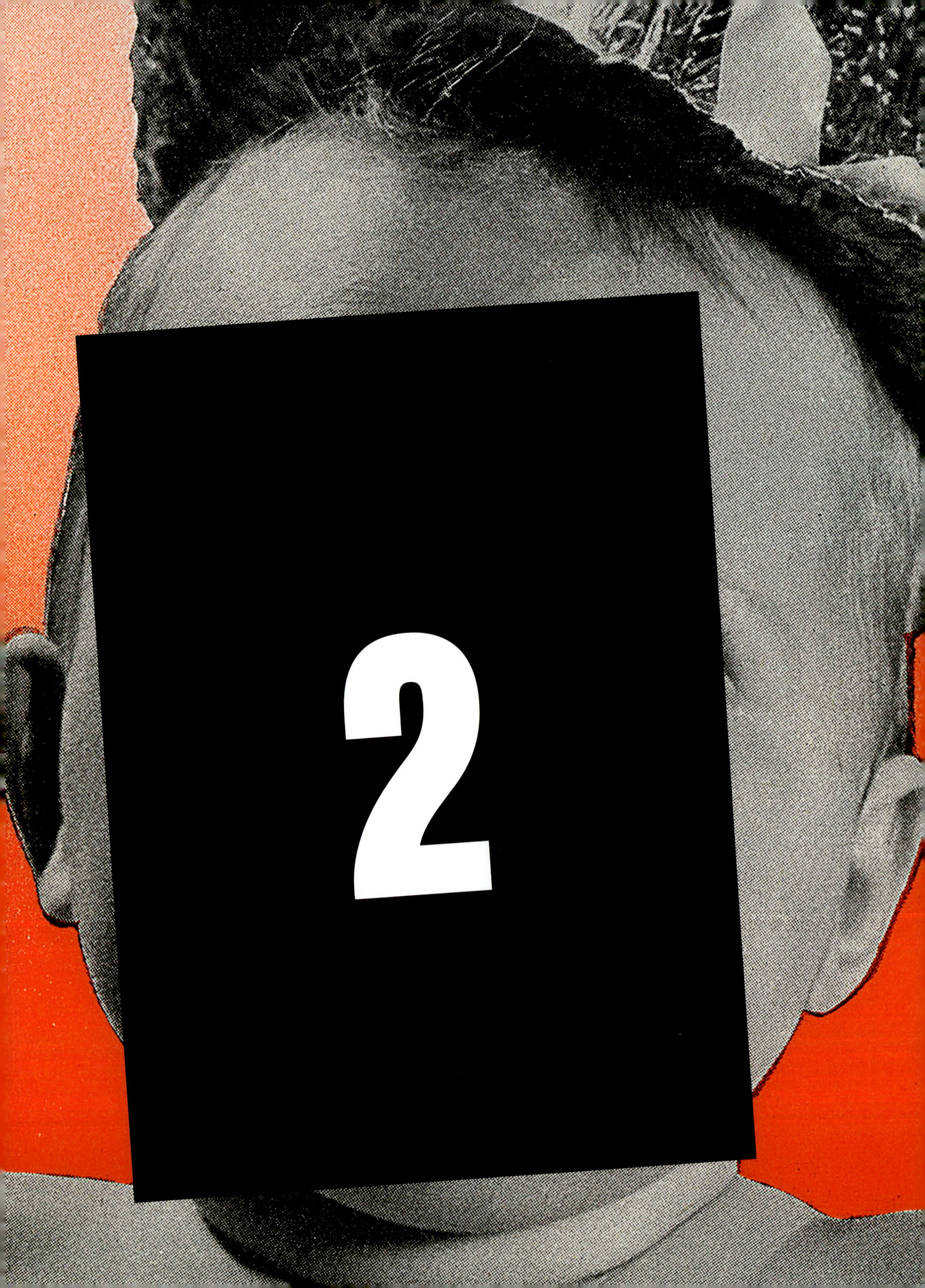
2

GEE,
MOMMY
YOU
SURE
ENJOY
YOUR
MARLBORO...

Lucky Strike, Lord, Thomas & Logan Agency, 1929

When tempted to overindulge
reach for a Lucky instead...

The tobacco giants won over
American men by introducing free
packets of cigarettes to C-rations for
US troops during World War I.

Few women smoked, and at the turn
of the century the only ladies to
light up in public were prostitutes.
The very act of smoking was seen
to be indicative of a low moral fibre.

Marketeers stayed away from a
female target audience for the first
decades of the twentieth century,
as calls grew for a ban on alcohol.

They feared that appeals to women
would focus the temperance
movement onto their product.

When Prohibition became
increasingly unpopular, cigarette
companies grew bolder in their
tactics to sell to the half of the
population who weren't yet smokers.

Edward Bernays, the father of the PR industry, was behind a campaign to establish that women smoking was socially acceptable.

In his campaigns cigarettes were 'torches of freedom', emancipating women with the right to enjoy smoking.

During the Easter Parade in New York of 1929 he hired hundreds of women to smoke as they made their way down 5th Avenue; this canny move linked women and tobacco and brought it into public life within a year.

One advertising strategy initially aimed at a female audience was to claim that smoking would help keep you thin and trim.

Launched in 1928, Lucky Strike promised a slender figure to women who decided that they would 'Reach for a Lucky instead of a sweet'.

The companies traded on the fact that cigarettes suppress the appetite, and so targeted women's sensitivity to gaining weight.

Their 1929 campaign featured Lady Grace Drummond-Hay, a British writer who was the first woman to fly around the world in a Zeppelin.

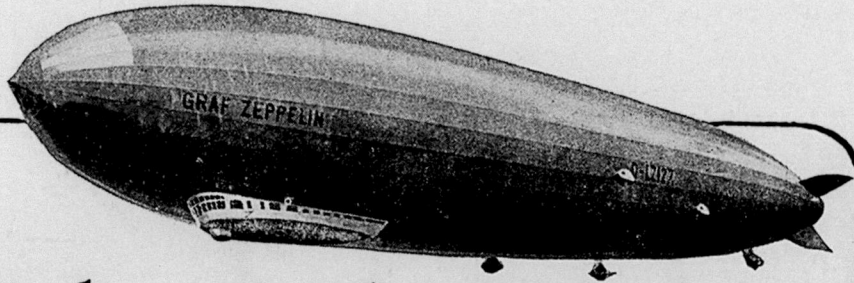

Lady Grace reported from the craft to various American newspapers, glamourising both aviation and the Zeppelin, and doing the same for Lucky Strike. 'I smoke a Lucky instead of eating sweets – that's what many men have been doing for years. I think it's high time we women smoked Luckies and kept our figures trim.'

These campaigns were eventually derailed by the sweet manufacturer's lobby.

As was the case with much tobacco advertising at the time, the product could be presented as being beneficial to all potential consumers.

Men were also stalked by the shadow of a future flabby self unless they smoked. 'Face the Facts, When Tempted to Over-Indulge, Reach for a Lucky Instead.'[77]

What would keep women slim would also keep men athletic and masculine.

A perfect product indeed.

And only in the world of marketing could the same advertising agencies that were promoting cigarettes as a way to stay thin, be simultaneously producing campaigns advising women that being skinny robbed you of any sex appeal.

Lucky Strike, Lord, Thomas & Logan Agency, 1930

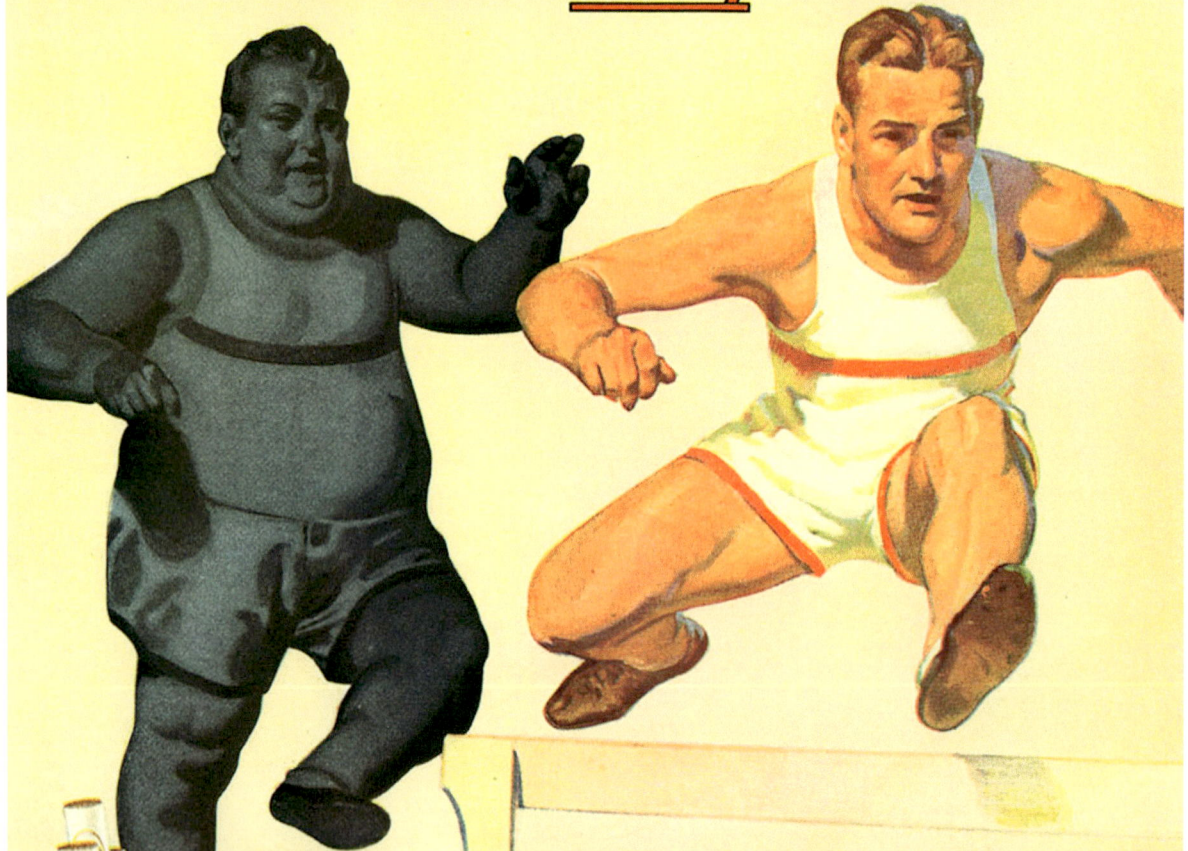

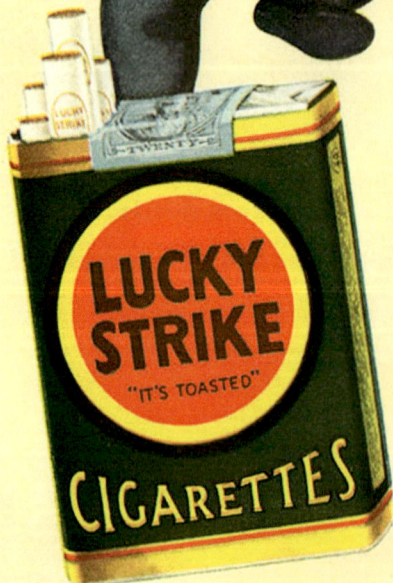

Lucky Strike, Lord, Thomas & Logan Agency, 1930

Lucky Strike was the best-selling
cigarette in America during the 1930s.

Using the slogan 'It's toasted', it
claimed to be more flavourful than
other cigarettes, which used tobacco
that was merely sun-dried.

In the first year of their suggesting you
'Reach for a Lucky instead of a sweet',
sales of the brand increased by 300%.

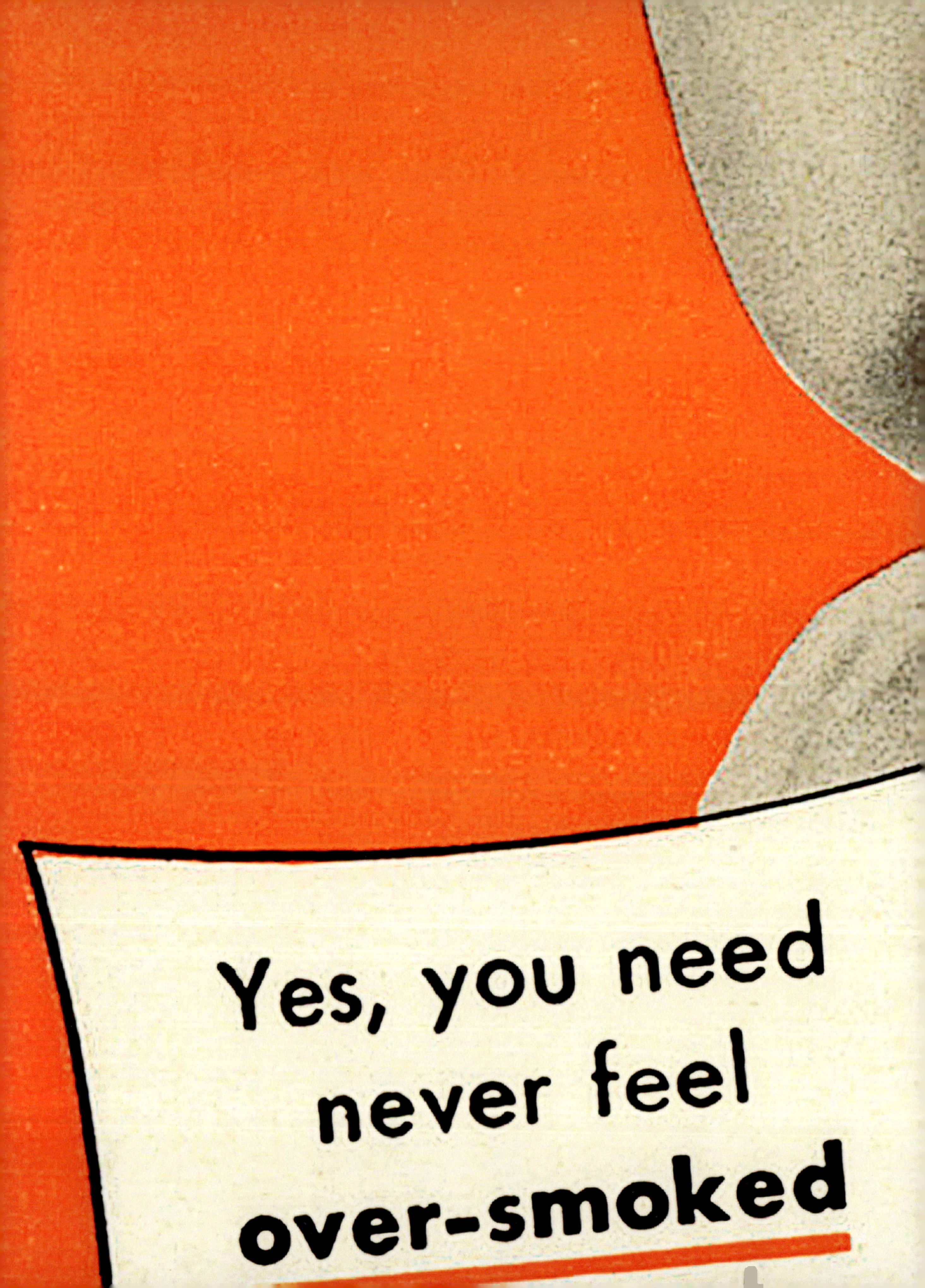

Yes, you need
never feel
over-smoked

IVORY TIPPED

MARLBO

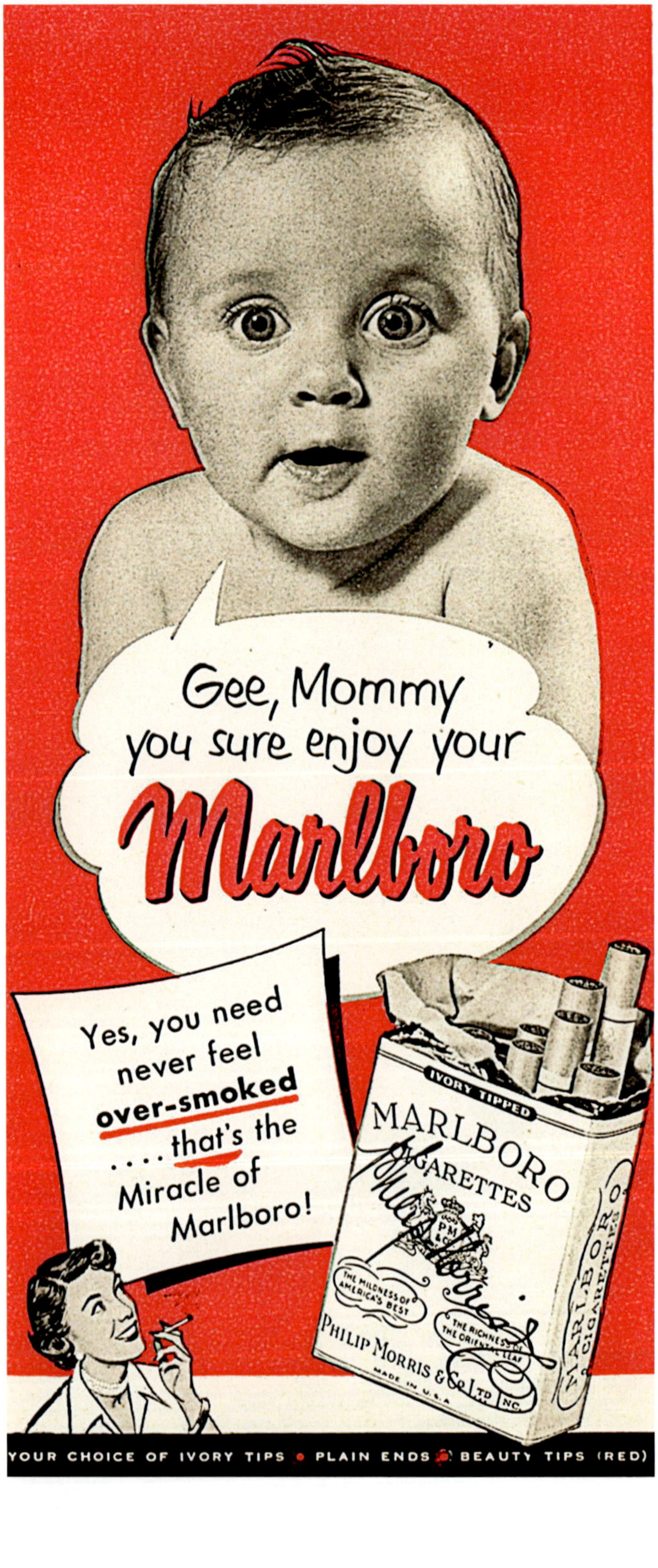

Marlboro, Milton Biow Agency, 1951

Before you scold me mom...

Post-War America and Europe
experienced an unprecedented
baby boom.

Preying on this growing fascination
with children, and their new
abundance, Marlboro released
a colourful campaign in 1951,
featuring 'talking babies'.

Alarming to the contemporary eye,
using infants as a central component
of the marketing strategy worked
to further establish smoking as a
family activity open to both men
and women, fathers and mothers,
at home and in public.

The synonymous values that babies stand for – youth, health and innocence – played well with Marlboro's bold approach.

By adopting the voice of the child itself, the brand addressed the core concern of new parents: what does my child want and how best can I care for it?

Smoking here is central to keeping baby happy, appealing to the calming effects of cigarettes 'Before you scold me, Mom…maybe you'd better light up a Marlboro'.

The voice also appeals to the male sense of pride: 'Gee Dad, you always get the best of everything…'

Before you scold me, Mom...
maybe you'd better light up a

Marlboro

Yes, you need never feel **over-smoked** — that's the Miracle of Marlboro!

IVORY TIPPED

MARLBORO CIGARETTES

THE MILDNESS OF AMERICA'S BEST
THE RICHNESS OF THE ORIENTAL LEAF

PHILIP MORRIS & Co. Ltd. Inc.
MADE IN U.S.A.

YOUR CHOICE OF IVORY TIPS • PLAIN ENDS • BEAUTY TIPS (RED)

Marlboro, Milton Biow Agency, 1951

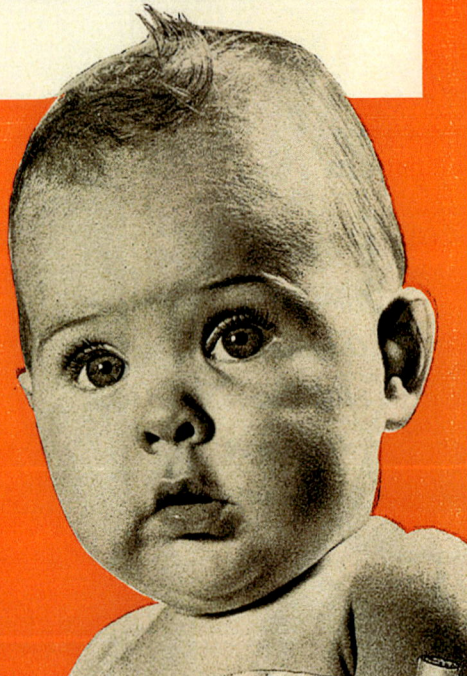
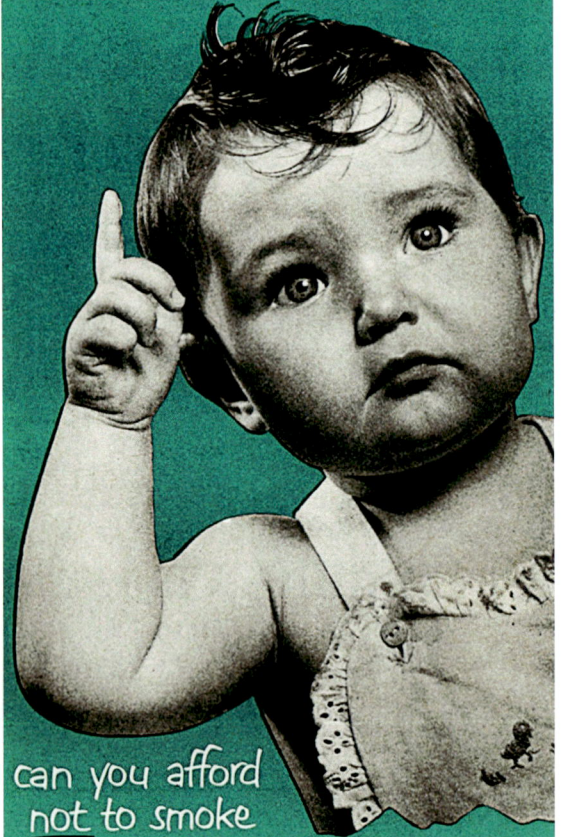

Marlboro, Milton Biow Agency, 1951

In the 1950s Marlboro switched
advertising agencies to Leo Burnett,
and in 1957 Marlboro Man was born.

The images in the ads were of craggy-
faced cowboys, seen with a cigarette in
their mouths in the forefront of scenic
Western landscapes.

They were conceived as a way to help
filtered cigarettes, which were
considered feminine, gain a more
rugged image.

The Marlboro Cowboy or Marlboro
Country campaigns ran for three
decades, and continue to be used in
Japan and the Far East.

How MILD can a cigarette be?

NOTED THROAT SPECIALISTS REPORT ON 30-DAY TEST OF CAMEL SMOKERS...

Not one single case of throat irritation due to smoking

Camels

Yes, these were the findings of noted throat specialists after a total of 2,470 weekly examinations of the throats of hundreds of men and women who smoked Camels — and only Camels — for 30 consecutive days.

GLAMOROUS PRIMA DONNA... Beautiful Patrice Munsel made her New York debut in opera at the age of 18...thrills concert and radio audiences with her soaring high C's...makes records treasured by music lovers.

66 **My career depends on my voice. I smoke cool, mild Camels—the cigarette that agrees with my throat!** 99

Patrice Munsel

CONCERT AND OPERA STAR

"Singing opera can put a strain on any voice. That's why I had to be *sure* my cigarette suited my throat! My own 30-Day Camel Mildness Test gave me the proof I needed.

"Smoking Camels day after day gave me plenty of time to decide on Camel mildness. I didn't have to make up my mind on a quick-trick, one-puff test or on a single sniff. I enjoyed Camels' rich flavor—pack after pack. They're such fun to smoke!"

MORE DOCTORS SMOKE CAMELS
than any other cigarette!

In a recent nationwide survey, doctors in every branch of medicine were asked what cigarette they smoked. The brand named most was Camel!

Make your own 30-Day Camel MILDNESS Test in your "T-Zone"

(T for Throat, T for Taste)

R. J. Reynolds Tobacco Company, Winston-Salem, N. C.

Camel, William Esty Agency, 1951

Not one single case of throat irritation...

Cigarette campaigns openly addressed health concerns.

The reccurring complaint that many cigarette brands sought to alleviate was the 'irritated throat'.

Ironically, their relentless pursuit of this issue was the result of widespread fears about smokers' cough.

One brand, Lucky Strike, had a particular approach to throat issues, proclaiming their 'toasted' cigarettes offered the best formula to soothe the condition.[71–77]

At the time tuberculosis, or consumption as it was then known, was rife and the public were concerned that tobacco workers would cough over the cigarettes they were making and so spread the disease to the consumer.

'Toasted' suggested that the heating process would destroy such germs, making Lucky Strikes safe and delicious.

Emotional health was also a powerful message employed by a number of brands.

In a campaign from Camel in 1955 celebrity endorsement was used to demonstrate that smoking creates well-being.

Using movie stars like John Wayne and Rock Hudson, the pleasures of smoking were framed as a way to improve your entire psychological state.

It would lessen the likelihood that you lose your temper, and would help us make calmer, better husbands, wives, parents and citizens.

Celebrity endorsement was a key factor in cigarette advertising campaigns, encouraging consumers to behave as their screen icons did.

IT'S A PSYCHOLOGICAL FACT: PLEASURE HELPS YOUR DISPOSITION

How's your disposition today?

IT'S NATURAL TO FEEL GRUMPY AS A GOAT when little annoyances pile up. But it's a psychological fact that pleasure helps your disposition. That means everyday pleasures are important. So, if you're a smoker, you should choose the cigarette that gives you the *most pleasure*. And that means *Camels* — America's most popular cigarette.

For more pure pleasure_have a Camel

John Wayne "I've been getting pleasure from Camels for over 20 years. You don't find that flavor and mildness in any other brand!"

Teresa Wright "It has the most delightful richness and mildness of any cigarette. You'll be as enthusiastic about Camels' pure pleasure as I am!"

Alan Ladd "I've tried them all and I'd still walk a mile for a Camel! For flavor and mildness, Camels agree best with me!"

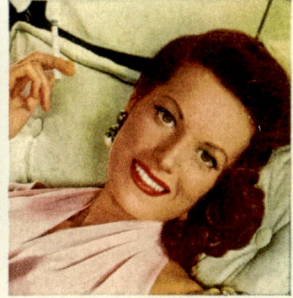

Maureen O'Hara "I found it's true — no other cigarette is so genuinely mild, yet so wonderfully rich-tasting as Camel!"

Brian Keith "I've tried many brands; now I know why they say, 'Once a Camel smoker, always a Camel smoker'."

Joanne Dru "There just isn't that richer flavor in any other brand but Camels. And they're definitely cool, smooth and mild!"

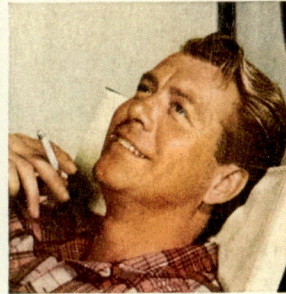

Gene Nelson "Since I switched to Camels, I've enjoyed smoking more. Nothing compares to Camels for pure pleasure, pack after pack."

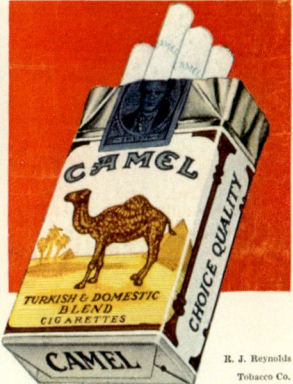

R. J. Reynolds Tobacco Co. Winston-Salem, N. C.

No other cigarette is so rich-tasting, yet so mild!

Singers were especially favoured
as their voice was their craft; Frank
Sinatra appeared in Chesterfield
adverts on TV and in print.

Often actors and actresses would
appear in advertising for more than
one brand.

Their support was dictated by deals
set up by individual studios making
a star's current movie.

Joan Crawford appeared in
advertisements for no less than
6 different brands.

The semiotics of tobacco advertising
developed over time.

'Mild' became a key word, suggesting
that such cigarettes weren't harmful,
and were demonstrated as better for
you by the '30 day Mildness Test'.

This in turn was replaced by 'light',
and more contemporary cigarettes
were later positioned as 'ultra-light'.

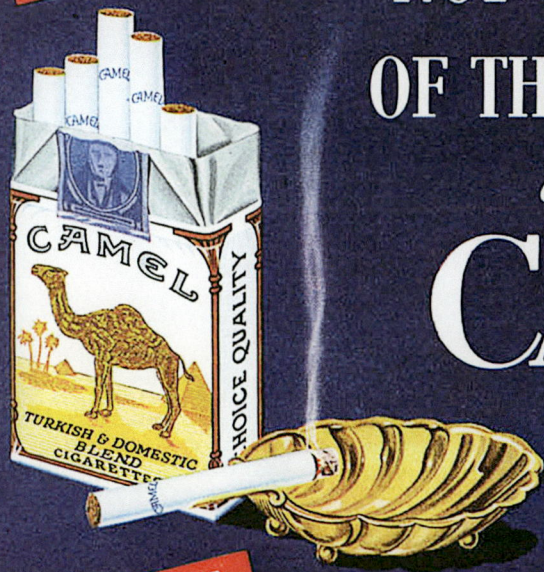

30-DAY TEST REVEALED

NOT ONE SINGLE CASE
OF THROAT IRRITATION
due to smoking
CAMELS!

DOCTORS REPORT

Yes, that's what noted throat specialists reported after making weekly examinations of the throats of hundreds of people, from coast to coast, who smoked Camels, and only Camels, for 30 consecutive days!

SMOKERS REPORT

MRS. ARTHUR O'NEILL, housewife: "I made the Camel 30-Day Test and enjoyed every puff of it! For taste *and* flavor, it's Camels every time!"

STEEL WORKER Cyril Byrne: "On my job, a good cigarette is a good friend. I made the 30-Day Test—now Camels are my smoke for keeps!"

LOVELY SOCIALITE Mrs. Thomas Phipps: "My search for a milder, better-tasting cigarette is over! The test won me to Camels, and *only* Camels!"

COLE PORTER, famous song writer: "The doctors' report *proves* what I've known about Camels for years. They're as *mild* as they are *flavorful!*"

TELEPHONE OPERATOR Rita Edwards: "The 30-Day Test really convinced me! Camels are the mildest, best-tasting cigarette I've ever smoked!"

WILLIE HOPPE, master of the cue: "30 Days? My personal test of Camels covers 20 years. I *know* how good Camels taste! I *know* how mild Camels are!"

JINX CLARK, lovely show-skater: "I put Camels to the test in my 'T-Zone'. There's nothing quite like them for flavor. And Camels are so wonderfully mild!"

STOREKEEPER Bernard Unger: "By my test, Camels are a standout for flavor! And they're *mild*. I know . . . I smoke over a pack a day. It's Camels for me!"

BOBSLED ACE Francis Tyler: "I'm talking from experience when I say Camels are mild. I've smoked them for years. And Camels sure *taste* great!"

STAR AQUA-SKIER Margie Fletcher: "Looks like I'll be stretching the 30-Day Test into many happy years of smoking Camels! They suit me to a 'T'!"

Make your own
Camel 30-Day Test in your "T-Zone"

● Over and beyond the reports of noted throat specialists, the final authority on Camel mildness and flavor is your own "T-Zone" (T for taste, T for throat). Test Camels yourself for 30 days. See how your taste appreciates the rich, full flavor of Camel's choice tobaccos. See what your throat reports on Camel's cool mildness. See if *you, too*, don't change to Camels for keeps!

Noted throat specialists report on 30-day test of Camel smokers . . .

NOT ONE SINGLE CASE OF THROAT IRRITATION *due to smoking* CAMELS!

Yes, these were the findings of noted throat specialists after a total of 2,470 weekly examinations of the throats of hundreds of men and women who smoked Camels— and only Camels—for 30 consecutive days.

THE TEST WAS REALLY FUN! EVERY CAMEL TASTED SO GOOD! AND I DIDN'T NEED MY DOCTOR'S REPORT TO KNOW CAMELS ARE **MILD**!

ELANA O'BRIAN, real estate broker, one of the hundreds of people from coast to coast who made the 30-Day Test of Camel Mildness under the observation of noted throat specialists.

. . . AND THOUSANDS MORE AGREE!

Start your own 30-Day Camel MILDNESS *Test Today!*

It's fun—it's enlightening! All you do is smoke Camels, and only Camels, for 30 days. Compare them in your "T-Zone" (T for taste, T for throat). See if that rich, full Camel flavor and that cool, cool Camel mildness doesn't win you to Camels for keeps.

CAMEL
TURKISH & DOMESTIC BLEND CIGARETTES

R. J. Reynolds Tobacco Co., Winston-Salem, N. C.

"CAMELS AGREE with my throat—and they sure taste great!" says Ed Paxton, chemical engineer, who made the Camel 30-day test under a throat specialist.

EDITORIAL ASSISTANT Virginia Walcutt: "I didn't believe any cigarette could smoke so mild. But Camels met the test—they certainly agree with my throat!"

"I'M A VETERAN when it comes to smoking Camels. They give me the kind of smoke I like—lots of flavor and plenty mild!" Michael Douglas, singer.

MISS LEE TELLER, secretary: "I'm delighted that I made the 30-day mildness test. It introduced me to the cigarette that really agrees with my throat—Camels!"

"THE 30-DAY TEST was a real education. It taught me that there's no cigarette quite like a Camel!" Tod Crone, air travel agency owner.

SPORTSWOMAN Jean French: "I like to make my own tests; I smoked Camels for 30 days. They tasted so good I've changed to Camels for keeps!"

In 1956 Phillip Morris launched its 'Born Gentle' series aimed at young women.[98]

The advertisements showed a mother and her newborn, equating the tenderness of maternal love with the mild softness of the Phillip Morris brand.

With copy reading 'Young mothers, please forgive us if we too feel something of the pride of a new parent,' they directly addressed a specific target audience, the young breast-feeding mother.

As health concerns grew, Old Gold attempted to buck the trend of justifying smoking through its medicinal benefits.[97]

They played once again with the pleasure principal of smoking, with a showgirl's legs protruding from a packet – this brand 'gives you a treat instead of a treatment'.

Old Gold, J. Walter Thompson Agency, 1950

Born gentle

Proud mothers, please forgive us if we too feel something of the pride of a new parent. For new Philip Morris, today's Philip Morris, is delighting smokers everywhere. Enjoy the gentle pleasure, the *fresh unfiltered flavor*, of this new cigarette, born gentle, then refined to special gentleness in the making. Ask for new Philip Morris in the smart new package.

©1956, Philip Morris Inc.

New Philip Morris...*gentle for modern taste*

Philip Morris
Cigarettes

PHILIP MORRIS Inc NEW YORK

King Size
or
Regular
Snap-open
Pack

Philip Morris, Leo Burnett Agency, 1957

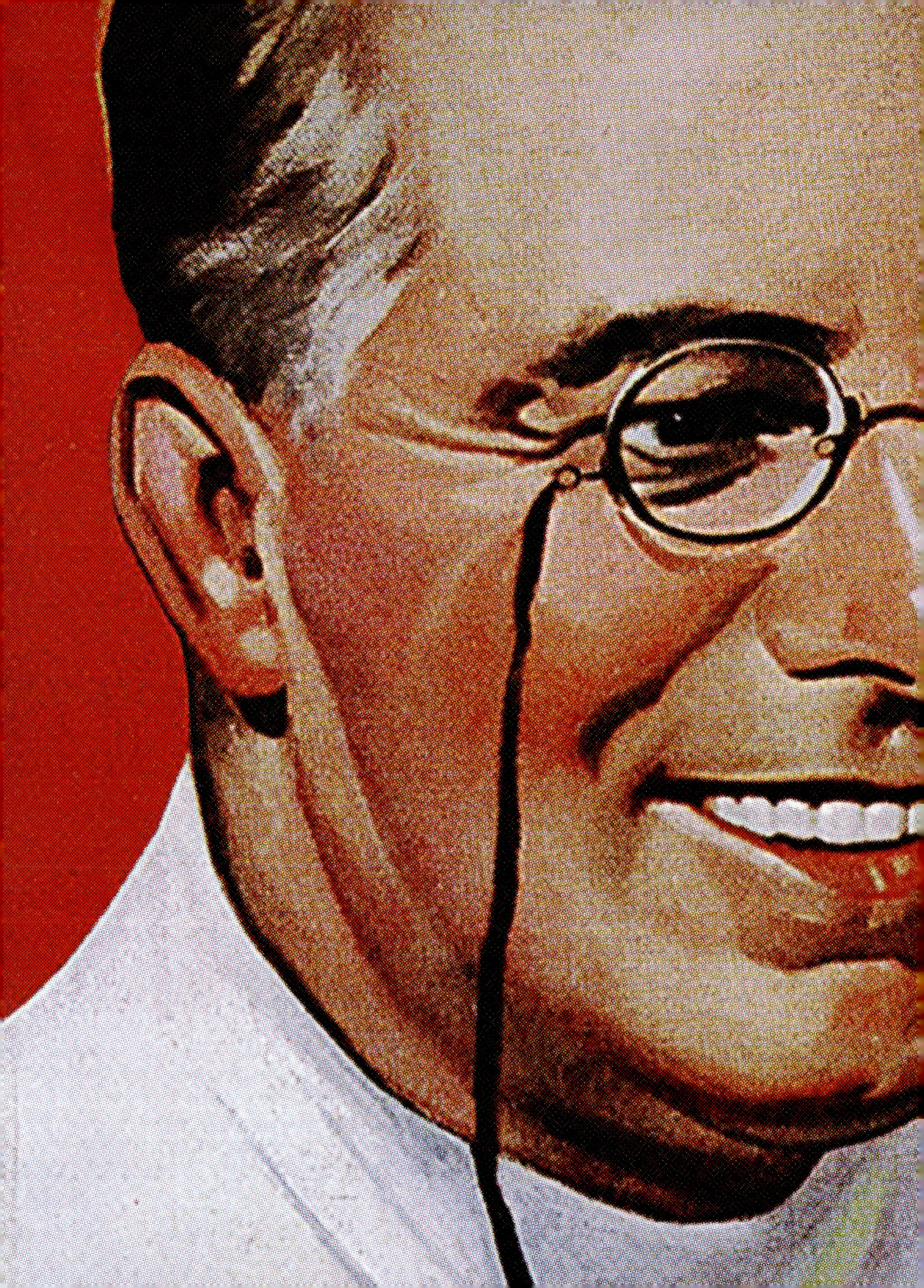

"I'm going to grow a hundred years old!"

...and possibly she may — for the amazing strides of medical science have added years to life expectancy

● It's a fact — a warm, wonderful fact — that this five-year-old child, or your own child, has a life expectancy almost a whole decade longer than was her mother's, and a good 18 to 20 years longer than that of her grandmother. Not only the expectation of a longer life, but of a life by far healthier.

Thank medical science for that. Thank your doctor and thousands like him... toiling ceaselessly... that you and yours may enjoy a longer, better life.

According to a recent Nationwide survey:

More Doctors smoke Camels
than any other cigarette!

NOT ONE but three outstanding independent research organizations conducted this survey. And they asked not just a few thousand, but 113,597, doctors from coast to coast to name the cigarette they themselves preferred to smoke.

Answers came in by the thousands... from general physicians, diagnosticians, surgeons, nose and throat specialists too. The most-named brand was Camel.

If you are not now smoking Camels, try them. Let your "T-Zone" tell you *(see right).*

R. J. Reynolds Tobacco Co., Winston-Salem, N. C.

CAMELS *Costlier Tobaccos*

CAMEL TURKISH & DOMESTIC BLEND CIGARETTES

THE "T-ZONE" TEST WILL TELL YOU

The "T-Zone"—T for taste and T for throat —is your own proving ground for any cigarette. Only your taste and throat can decide which cigarette tastes best to you... how it affects your throat.

Camel, William Esty Agency, 1950

Scientists, Doctors, Educators and Santa Claus...

In the battle to enlist entire populations to smoke, no respectable public figure was left untried as a spokesperson.

The concerns about the medical effects of smoking were vocal enough to make phrases like 'smoker's cough' and 'coffin nails' become part of the language. The marketeers' reaction? Bring in the men in white coats.

The most widespread of these campaigns featured the most respected pillar of the community, your local GP.

Unlike celebrity endorsements, these advertisements never featured actual physicians; they would be struck off were they to engage in promotional activity.

However, the medical world had a cosy relationship with the American tobacco giants. At American Medical Association conferences there would be cigarette-sponsored salons where doctors could pick up their free packets of cigarettes, the cartons of which would be monogrammed with their initials.

The claims made in Camel adverts, 'More Doctors Smoke Camels Than Any Other Cigarette',[101] were not based on national surveys, but upon the results of questionnaires posed to doctors as they left such conferences.

Employees of Camel would stand on the door and ask each departing doctor which brand he had in his pocket. Lo and behold, it was Camels – they had just visited the Camel lounge to pick up their free packs.

Earlier advertising claimed '20,697 Physicians find Lucky Strike cigarettes less irritating'. The exactitude of this very specific number suggested the thoroughness of the research, as round numbers wouldn't.

Lucky Strike, Lord, Thomas & Logan Agency, 1930

ALL OVER AMERICA...
MORE SCIENTISTS AND EDUCATORS
SMOKE KENT with the MICRONITE FILTER
than any other cigarette!

For good smoking taste,
it makes good sense to smoke **KENT**

REGULAR-SIZE, KING-SIZE
OR CRUSH-PROOF BOX

A PRODUCT OF P. LORILLARD COMPANY · FIRST WITH THE FINEST CIGARETTES · THROUGH LORILLARD RESEARCH   © 1960, P. LORILLARD CO.

Kent, Young & Rubicam Agency, November 1960

Kent advertisements drew on other respected members of American society, the 'Scientist' and the 'Educator'. Cleverly pitching its message to middle class Americans, marketers traded on the respect and rationality of these figures to back-up a novel invention in tobacco – the filter tip.

Their 'micronite filter' is graphically demonstrated as being longer and better for you. Ironically, many of the filters employed at the time were made from asbestos.

The 'puff chart' employed by Pall Mall showed a similar 'scientific fact' – the longer the cigarette, the 'milder' the smoke becomes as you draw on the cigarette.[108]

Santa Claus, long a commercial figure whose merry hue of red was dictated by Coca-Cola, was again a useful tool in encouraging the young to smoke, and a way to popularise gifting cigarettes at Christmas.

And Father Christmas could be relied on to recommend a brand that wouldn't give you 'scratchy throat'.

Pall Mall claimed that their longer 'smooth' cigarette filtered the smoke and made it mild.

'Mild' was seen at the time as a code word meant to indicate a healthier smoke, and other cigarettes were to be considered as 'harsh'.

Their 'Puff Chart' diagram demonstrated that Pall Mall's extra length allowed more smoke to be filtered.

But the 'Throat-Scratch' campaign disappeared despite its great success, after the authorities decreed that it was misleading. They argued, rather logically, that a longer cigarette contained more tobacco and irritants; the Pall Mall brand lost momentum, and never found an effective alternative approach.

Guard Against Throat-Scratch

enjoy the smooth smoking of fine tobaccos

...smoke PALL MALL the cigarette whose mildness you can measure

PALL MALL
FAMOUS CIGARETTES

IN HOC SIGNO VINCES

Study This Puff Chart:

PUFF BY PUFF...YOU'RE ALWAYS AHEAD WITH PALL MALL

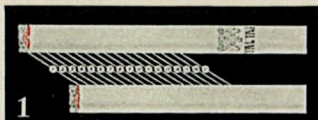

1 The further your cigarette filters the smoke through fine tobaccos, the milder that smoke becomes. At the first puff, PALL MALL's smoke is filtered further than that of any other leading cigarette.

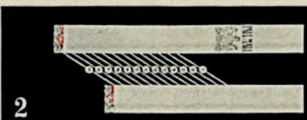

2 Again after 5 puffs of each cigarette your own eyes can measure the extra length for extra mildness as the smoke of PALL MALL's traditionally fine tobaccos is filtered further. Moreover, after 10 puffs of each cigarette ...

3 ... or 17 puffs, Pall Mall's greater length of fine tobaccos still travels the smoke further —filters the smoke and makes it mild. Thus Pall Mall gives you a smoothness, mildness and satisfaction no other cigarette offers you.

Wherever you go today, you will see more and more people smoking PALL MALL— the cigarette whose mildness you can measure.

Outstanding

...and they are mild !

P.S. LET A CARTON OF PALL MALLS SAY "MERRY CHRISTMAS" FOR YOU

Copr. 1951, American Cigarette and Cigar Co., Inc.

Pall Mall, Sullivan, Stauffer, Colwell & Bayles Agency, 1951

on!

th. Casual

3

Rumor has it that even he

FOLKS
JUS'
CAN'T
HELP
HAVIN'
A
FRIENDLY
FEELIN'
FOR
DIS
HEAH
COFFEE...

Golly, Mis' Maria

FOLKS JUS' CAN'T HELP HAVIN' A FRIENDLY FEELIN' FOR DIS HEAH COFFEE!

Molasses and January—the boys who "tote aroun'" the coffee to all the Show Boat guests—know what people think of Maxwell House Coffee!

Smiles of satisfaction always greet the mellow, rich, full-bodied goodness that's in every cup of this fine coffee.

For Maxwell House has *everything* that goes to make a coffee delicious ...

It is the same matchless blend of choice coffees that the aristocrats of the Old South knew and loved many years ago. No other blend has ever quite compared for rich, satisfying flavor.

ROASTER-FRESH ALWAYS

It brings you, too, the fragrant freshness of the roasting ovens. Packed by the exclusive Vita-Fresh process, Maxwell House always comes to you as fresh and full-flavored as the very hour it was scooped warm from the roaster. And no coffee can be fresher than that!

And it is ground by a newly developed process that assures you perfect uniformity and delicious flavor in every cup

of coffee ... whether you make it by the drip, percolator or any other method.

Why don't you try Maxwell House Coffee today? We think you too will be delighted with the smooth, delicious flavor of this famous blend.

And you'll find the price surprisingly low. Millions have learned that it costs no more, in fact, than many coffees of lower quality standards. Maxwell House Coffee is a product of General Foods. It is always Good to the Last Drop.

★ FRESH AS THE HOUR IT LEFT THE ROASTER ★ A BLEND THE YEARS HAVE NEVER MATCHED

MOLASSES AND JANUARY stop their fun-making long enough to pour "another cup of coffee" for Maria, Captain Henry's sister. Hear these stars of the Maxwell House Show Boat—one of radio's greatest shows—every Thursday night. Hear, also, the lovely voices of Lanny Ross, Annette Hanshaw, Conrad Thibault and Mary Lou, and the glorious music of Don Voorhees and his Show Boat Band. A full hour of gorgeous entertainment—every Thursday night! N.B.C. Coast-to-Coast hook-up. © G. F. Corp., 1934

MAXWELL HOUSE ... GOOD TO THE LAST DROP

Ad No. M-3
Saturday Evening Post . . January 27, 1934
9 3-8 x 12 1-8 in. Final Proof, December 11, 1933

Maxwell House, Benton & Bowles Agency, 1934

The white man's burden...

Molasses and January, the two 'boys' pictured in the ad opposite from 1935, were characters starring in *Captain Henry's Maxwell House Show Boat*, the most popular radio programme in the US at the time.

They are seen here with Maria, another star of the show.

Maxwell House's advertising agency Benton & Bowles, had picked up on the popularity of radio entertainment and suggested that their client sponsor a show.

Thanks to extensive advertising throughout the 1920s, the product was already the most well-known coffee brand in the USA.

Their radio show featured various musical numbers, comedy sketches, and of course some cleverly integrated advertising – stars of the show backstage would casually talk among themselves (with the microphones on) about marvellous Maxwell House.

Captain Henry politely interrogates Tiny Ruffner, the radio announcer, so as not to seem too pushy to listeners,

Captain: 'Tiny, exactly what do you mean when you say that everybody who buys Maxwell House Coffee gets full value for their money?'

Tiny: 'Well, I refer to three separate things… firstly, for more than fifty years it's been the favourite of people who really enjoy good coffee.'

Captain: 'And our favourite as well!'

Tiny: 'Right you are, Captain Henry!'

Fashion's new favorite! Van Ron collar in Oxford cloth. New, soft, rounded collar, without stays.

The roll's the thing! Van Roll button-down spread in Oxford. Curves from neck to collar point.

College and alumni tradition! Button-down in Oxford cloth. Casual yet always dressy.

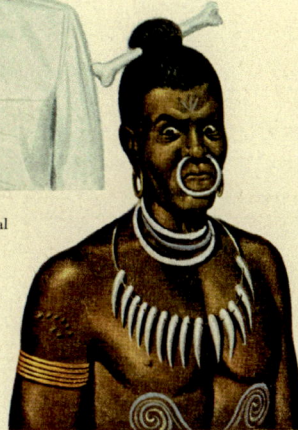

Rumor has it that even he would gladly swap his boar's teeth for a Van Heusen Oxford!

Style sensation! Van Roll collar in Oxford cloth . . . rolls as it spreads . . . for a more casual look.

4 out of 5 men want Oxfords ...in these new Van Heusen styles

Come in whites, colors and stripes. Only **$4.50**
A new shirt free if your Van Heusen shrinks out of size.
The ties: Van Heusen Oxford Shirtmates, $1.50
Phillips-Jones Corp., N.Y. 1, N.Y. Makers of Van Heusen Shirts • Sport Shirts
Ties • Pajamas • Handkerchiefs • Underwear • Swimwear • Collars
and the famous Van Heusen Century Shirt with the soft collar that won't wrinkle ever.

Van Heusen shirts
"the world's smartest" REG. T. M.

Molasses and January were in fact two Irishmen Pick Malone and Pat Padgett, vaudeville comics specialising in blackface, white performers disguised as black for comic value, a popular entertainment at the time.

Their acts were in the minstrel style, mainly improvised sketches working without a script, always 'wittily' insulting African Americans:

Molasses: 'What's up January, you look kinda down in the mouth?'

January: 'I've got t'walk backwards to keep from walkin' on my lips!'

Blackface actors traditionally used burnt cork to blacken their faces, with exaggerated noses and lips painted red or white, similar to a circus clown's wide smile today.

No ma'am!
no vermins in *my* kitchen

I DON' hol' wid 'em. I don' believe in 'em, nor yit I don' intend to fool along wid 'em.

De first one dar' show his bowdacious head, I shoots 'im wid Flit. In de ole days, I used for to bash 'em wid an iron, an' sometimes I hits him an' sometimes I misses him. Wid Flit I sholy gits him.

Yas'm, Miss Lucy she says to me, "Shoot 'em wid Flit."

I 'sponds,

"What in de worl' am dat?"

Miss Lucy, she 'sponds,

"Dat Flit am a liquid in a gun which is gwine to gas 'em. It don'

do no harm to no human, but it sho' do 'nihilate dem bugs."

No, I ain't trouble wid no vermin 'cause I do like Miss Lucy say. I shoots 'em wid Flit. I shoots de great ones an' I shoots de small ones. De daddies an' de mammies of every kin' of bugs. Flies, 'skeetos, ants, roaches. I slays 'em. I keeps de gun right handy. 'Tain't no

trouble 't all. Dat little easy contraption do de wuk of six of dem giggling house gals in de ole days.

No ma'am, mos' times I don' hol' wid changes. Half de time dat's all dey is—changes.

But dis yere Flit—dat's more'n a change. Hit's a 'provement.

———

Do not confuse Flit with ordinary insecticides. Greater killing power insures that Flit will give you complete satisfaction. Flit is made on honor by one of the largest corporations in the world.

It's Plastics Picking Time down South

How Chemistry Helps Create New Materials From Nature's Crops

Below Mason and Dixon's line, there's a drift of white across the map. Snowy cotton dapples fields that yesterday were waving green. Tomorrow, you will wear it as cloth, write on it as paper, put it to a thousand uses as plastics.

Plastics from *cotton?* Yes — from cotton, from wood pulp and from chemicals that have their genesis deep in the earth as coal and limestone, on the earth as corn, above the earth as elements of the very air itself. To these basic elements, Chemistry adds its acids, plasticizers and solvents, while Industry provides its scientific processes and its craftsmanship.

The result? A flood of man-made materials un-dreamed of a generation ago, bringing new articles of universal usefulness. The fountain pen with which these words were written, the typewriter keys on which they were copied, the frames of the glasses through which many are reading them—all owe their beauty, utility and low cost to *plastics*.

From steering wheels to hair ornaments, from transparent boxes to colorful radio cabinets, the list of products made from plastics is well-nigh endless.

Such is another service of Chemistry to Industry...helping produce new materials for a new age to better serve the needs of all mankind. MONSANTO CHEMICAL COMPANY, St. Louis.

HOW MONSANTO SERVES

Monsanto Chemical Company produces 31 chemical products used in the manufacture of plastics. In addition, its Plastics Division at Springfield, Massachusetts, produces these plastics:

**Cellulose Acetate • Cellulose Nitrate
Cast Phenolic Resin • Vinyl Acetals
Polystyrene • Resinox Phenolic Compounds**

Sheets • Rods • Tubes
**Molding Compounds • Castings
Vue-Pak Transparent Packaging Materials**

MONSANTO CHEMICALS
SERVING INDUSTRY...WHICH SERVES MANKIND

Monsanto Chemicals, Gardner Advertising Co. Agency, *Fortune,* 1939

Minstrel shows, and later the
vaudeville theatres which evolved
from them, included pastiches
of black music and dance, and
performers speaking in a 'plantation'
dialect.

Minstrel shows appeared to be a
way for Americans to separate
themselves culturally from their
European counterparts after the
war of independence, serving as the
United States alternative to opera.

As well as *Show Boat,* Maxwell
House sponsored the radio program
Father Knows Best, with each
episode beginning with the youngest
daughter Kitten asking: 'Mother, is
Maxwell House really the best coffee
in the whole world?' to which her
mother would reply, 'Well, your
father says so, and father knows best!'

The peak of popularity for minstrel
shows was 1830 to 1900, but lingered
on in radio and advertising.

It was customary for specific and
definitive racial stereotypes to be
called upon to market products.
Hellmann's[123] and Flit[116] seen here
made use of one such standby:
'Mammy'.

Mammy worked as a nanny for a family, and was usually unattractive to the Western eye: grossly overweight, with an over-ample bosom.

She is matronly, but maternal; strict, but with a tender hand; and considered non-threatening to white people, though tough and protective of her charges.

One notable Mammy was played by Hattie McDaniel in *Gone With The Wind*, who became the first African American to win an Oscar in 1939.

Because of their wholesome association with a happy home, Mammies in mainstream advertising were employed to market a whole array of household items, as well as cleaning products and food.

Another stereotype was the 'Uncle Tom': like Rastus of Cream of Wheat overleaf, they were faithful, happy and submissive servants used to create the illusion that Toms and Mammies were thoroughly content and loyal.[122]

The first step towards lightening

The White Man's Burden

is through teaching the virtues of cleanliness.

Pears' Soap

is a potent factor in brightening the dark corners of the earth as civilization advances, while amongst the cultured of all nations it holds the highest place—it is the ideal toilet soap.

When the J. Walter Thompson advertising agency took over the Cream of Wheat account in 1895 they suggested swapping the caricature of an African American man for a photograph of a real person.

This decision rapidly increased sales in the product, and the photo they chose has hardly changed from 1895 to today.

This man's name – Rastus – was commonly used at the time as a derogatory name for black men.

It is unclear why, as Rastus was not a popular name among African Americans, any more than white Americans.

The language in many of these advertisements is written in a plantation dialect, reinforcing the notion that a person who spoke in this way was uneducated or illiterate.

Cream of Wheat, *Needlecraft*, 1921

YAS, HONEY CHILD, DIS HEAH'S REAL MAYONNAISE !

Yo Mammy's Quality Folks—She Won't Serve Nuthin' Else.

"Folks like yo' mammy jus' knows dat those ordinary dressin's caint come up to Hellmanns Real Mayonnaise. Dey jus' don' have dat same wonderful flavour or rich creamy goodness!"

And there's a very simple explanation. Real mayonnaise like Hellmanns is made differently . . . with only choice salad oil, freshly-broken eggs, special vinegar and imported spices. No starchy fillers. And then it's *double-whipped* for creamy smoothness.

Why not get a jar of Hellmanns Mayonnaise—today? It costs but a trifle per salad . . . and makes those salads so much more delicious.

Picnic Sandwiches made with Best Foods

PEANUT BUTTER AND ONION—Blend ¼ cup Hellmanns Real Mayonnaise with 1 cup beaten peanut butter. Spread on bread, top with thin onion slices.

DEVILED EGG AND HAM—Blend thoroughly ¼ cup Hellmanns Real Mayonnaise; 2 finely chopped hard-boiled eggs; ½ cup devilled ham and 4 tablespoons diced Fanning's Bread and Butter Pickles. Spread on thinly sliced bread.

HELLMANN'S REAL MAYONNAISE

This literary tool was used to express a sense of superiority and share a snigger with the reader at the character's expense.

Here, Rastus expresses ignorance at what he's eating and even undermines the product by questioning its nutritional value, 'Maybe Cream of Wheat aint got no vitamines... but it sho is cheap!'

The Cream of Wheat image presents a puzzling picture to viewers – the tone of the man's writing suggests he is illiterate, yet he can write and is dressed in what appears to be a chef's white coat and hat, an educated and intelligent professional.

Van Heusen generally leaned towards the overtly sexist advertising seen in the first chapter of this book, but they also dabbled in a little casual racism.[114]

Sitting among four white, All-American men in various shades of pastel shirts, the savage tribesman glares at you – jealously we can only presume.

Monsanto are the corporation associated with being the first to promote genetically modified 'franken-foods' and creating Agent Orange.

Strangely, they decided that their advertisement for plastic products should portray a plantation with happy slave cotton pickers.[117]

They presented this idyllic image in an attempt to create an air of outdoorsy goodness, and instil a warm feeling towards the company.

Monsanto has since been embroiled in a number of damaging charges about its chemical products, and little public support seems to be forthcoming, despite their whimsical marketing initiative seen here.

The headline for the Pears' soap ad is taken from a Rudyard Kipling poem written in 1899:[120]

Take up the White Man's burden

Send forth the best ye breed

Go bind your sons to exile

To serve your captives' need;

To wait in heavy harness,

On fluttered folk and wild

Your new-caught, sullen peoples,

Half-devil and half-child.

In the poem Kipling calls out to America, which was at the time in the midst of a war with the Philippines, to stand up to their duty to civilise the more barbaric peoples of the world.

Perhaps he meant well; he certainly believed in encouraging colonisation, but describing the hapless recipients of his civilising largesse as 'sullen people, half-devil and half-children' was an unusual approach.

Pears' interpreted this poem to be about 'the virtues of cleanliness' and illustrated it with a tenacious, proudly moustached sea captain to represent Britain and America, and a sorry-looking, dirty native on a dismal beach to represent the burden.

"*I have found PEARS' SOAP matchless for the Hands and Complexion.*"

BY SPECIAL APPOINTMENT TO   H.R.H. THE PRINCE OF WALES.

FOR THE

COMPLEXION.

ESTABLISHED
1789

SOLD EVERYWHERE.

PURE,

FRAGRANT,

AND DURABLE.

Pears' Soap, A & F Pears Agency, 1884

You dirty boy...

A number of companies thought it amusing to suggest that products could whiten black skin.

Pears' Soap implied that their soap was so effective it could rid a black boy of his 'dirty' dark skin.

A sweet but puzzled white child innocently asks, 'why doesn't your mama wash you with Fairy Soap?'[133]

More grotesque was Chlorinol Soda,[136] which claimed that black boys could bleach themselves to become white, and equally charming was the Elliott paint advertisement which illustrated how well their white paint could cover black.[132]

They chose to illustrate this benefit by having a black child paint his friend with the product.

Vinolia Soap was probably the most repellent example of soap advertising that implied that black skin was unclean.[139]

An adorable looking white girl simply inquires of the unfortunate Dirty Boy 'why don't you wash with Vinolia?'

The offensiveness of so much of the advertising produced at this time is alarming.

Slavery had long been abolished and even though racism was still commonplace in the Deep South, civil rights campaigns were already pricking the public conscience by the 1930s.

"WHY DOESN'T YOUR MAMMA WASH YOU WITH FAIRY SOAP?"

Made only by THE N. K. FAIRBANK COMPANY.

CHICAGO, ST. LOUIS, NEW YORK, BOSTON, PHILADELPHIA, PITTSBURGH, BALTIMORE.

But apparently, in the boardrooms of America's corporations and their agencies, deeply racist advertising was considered acceptable, if presented in a light-hearted, folksy way.

But looking back today, nothing about them could be described as fondly jocular. Quite the reverse.

Soap in early advertisements represented the new middle-class values emerging in the West at the turn of the twentieth century, and a new fascination with cleanliness.

It was a time when certain virtues were considered important to uphold: monogamous 'clean' sex; Christian ideals; social barriers enforced; the Imperial mission of civilising and clothing the savages.

Soap was the very first commodity to be wrapped and sold using separate brand names in 1884, creating competition between vendors who had previously offered plain bars of soap, but were now identifying themselves as 'Pears' or 'Lifebuoy'.

Soap marketers liked to visualise themselves as 'empire builders' with 'the responsibility of the historic Imperial mission'.

Pears' particular advertising idea focused on the purifying of the working classes – maids, servants, menial workers and black children underwent magical transformations in their illustrations.

Soap was held in such high esteem that it was fetishised as an incredible product; maritime motifs were popular in the advertising to indicate the Empire and faraway lands.

Marketers only used black children in the ads, not adults, illustrating the point that the West considered the unfortunate condition of savagery as being identical to the condition of infancy.

Or as Kipling expressed it, 'half-devil and half-child'.

4

You can mask

No Halloween mask

SOCIETY SIMPLY WON'T STAND FOR INDELICATE WOMEN...

She was a "Perfect Wife"
...except for ONE NEGLECT*

She was lovely ... always took care to *look* smart and fresh.

... **efficient.** Her house was always neat, clean, well-run.

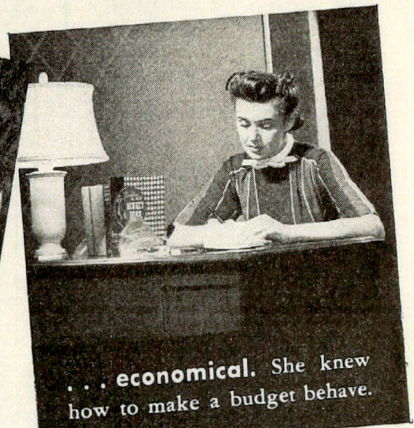

... **economical.** She knew how to make a budget behave.

... **affectionate.** She was warm-hearted and tender.

.... **cheerful.** She never nagged, or moped, or wept.

BUT ... she was careless (*or ignorant*) about Feminine Hygiene *And her husband would gladly have traded most of her virtues to correct this one fault.

"Lysol" might have made her score 100%

LOVE is not logical, more's the pity. You probably know at least one woman who seems to "have everything" *except the love of her husband.*

Don't be too sure he's just ungrateful ... Perhaps *she's* guilty of the one neglect no husband can stand. A neglect, a fault, that may kill a man's love, even when everything else is perfect.

If *you're* in any doubt about feminine hygiene—ask your doctor about "Lysol". Probably no other product is so widely known and used by women for this purpose. Here are some of the reasons why "Lysol" is preferred ...

1—Non-Caustic ... "Lysol" in the proper dilution, is gentle and efficient, contains no harmful free caustic alkali.

2—Effectiveness ... "Lysol" is a powerful *germicide*, active under practical conditions, effective in the presence of organic matter (such as dirt, mucus, serum, etc.).

3—Spreading ... "Lysol" solutions *spread* because of low surface tension, and thus virtually *search out germs.*

4—Economy ... "Lysol" is concentrated, costs only about one cent an application in the proper dilution for feminine hygiene.

5—Odor ... The cleanly odor of "Lysol" disappears after use.

6—Stability ... "Lysol" keeps its full strength no matter how long it is kept, how often it is uncorked.

Also, try Lysol Hygienic Soap for bath, hands and complexion. It's cleansing, deodorant.

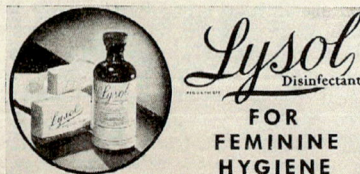

Lysol
Disinfectant
FOR FEMININE HYGIENE

What Every Woman Should Know
SEND COUPON FOR "LYSOL" BOOKLET
LEHN & FINK Products Corp.
Dept. H-903,   Bloomfield, N. J., U.S.A.
Send me free booklet "Lysol vs. Germs" which tells the many uses of "Lysol".

Name_____

Street_____

City_____ State_____
Copyright 1939 by Lehn & Fink Products Corp.

Lysol, Lehn & Fink Agency, *Hollywood*, 1939

A jewel with just one flaw...

Lysol Disinfectant began being marketed as a feminine hygiene product in the 1920s.

Vaginal douching using Lysol was claimed to prevent vaginal odour and infections.

Many of the advertisements suggest that women were repulsing their husbands with pungently malodorous vaginas, caused by neglected feminine hygiene.

Its ingredients were highly corrosive, and its formula more potent than today's Lysol, one of the leading household cleansers.

Lysol was marketed in a number of ways, and despite being promoted as a germicide, effective at cleaning toilet bowls and treating ringworm, it was simultaneously advertised for women's 'dainty feminine allure'.

This was commonly understood to be a euphemism for birth control, as it was widely believed that post-coital use of Lysol would prevent pregnancy.

In the first half of the twentieth century most women had limited access to other contraceptive methods or reliable medical knowledge.

Devices like diaphragms and condoms were expensive, and women increasingly turned to Lysol to stay baby-free, until 1960 when the oral contraceptive pill arrived.

Lysol killed a number of women – but not any sperm.

It was wholly ineffective as a contraceptive.

Clearly it also traded on female insecurities, suggesting to a woman that if her husband is cool towards her, it is the fault of her poor hygiene, and that she was to blame for marital disharmony.

Essentially Lysol won sales with a strategy that jeopardised women's health – claiming to be 'safe and gentle' for a woman to douche with, and yet powerful enough to be a robust, household cleaning disinfectant.

Today the thought of placing the now much milder Lysol anywhere near genitalia would make anyone wince.

Another Love-match *Shipwrecked*...

...on the dangerous reef of half-truths about feminine hygiene. "Lysol" has prevented many such tragedies.

Lysol, Lehn & Fink Agency, *Modern Screen*, December 1936

The bewildering fact about Lysol,
despite its claim of a plethora
of remedies for any kind of
gynaecological need, is that it is
a caustic poison.

Application to the skin, in the way
many American women had been
doing for decades, routinely caused
a 'burning itchiness' and
occasionally a 'severe inflammation'.

After a number of fatalities, the
American Medical Association
stepped in, and its genital use
was eradicated.

The failing company was then
acquired by a multinational
corporation; Lysol today is a market
leader once more with wide variety
of household cleansers and
disinfectant wipes, still using the
familiar Lysol scroll-lettered logo.

She was a Jewel of a Wife...*with just one flaw*

She was guilty of the "ONE NEGLECT"

that mars many marriages..."LYSOL" helps avoid this

EVERYONE admitted that Mary was beautiful, charming . . . a perfect housekeeper, cook, and mother. Why should her marriage have turned out badly?

She had failed in just one thing. One neglect had robbed her of the daintiness her husband loved. Do YOU use "Lysol" for intimate cleanliness?

Even the most tolerant husband finds it difficult to forget or forgive a wife's carelessness about feminine hygiene. More women should follow the "Lysol" method. "Lysol" is used by thousands of doctors, nurses, clinics, hospitals. Probably no other preparation has been so widely used by generations of women for feminine hygiene. "Lysol" is preferred because...

6 Special Features of "LYSOL"

1. Non-Caustic..."Lysol", in proper dilution, is gentle, efficient; contains no free caustic alkali. **2. Effectiveness**..."Lysol" is a powerful *germicide*, active under practical conditions; effective in the presence of organic matter (dirt, mucus, serum, etc.). **3. Spreading**... "Lysol" solutions *spread* because of low surface tension; virtually *search out germs*. **4. Economy** . . . Small bottle of "Lysol" makes almost 4 gallons of solution for feminine hygiene. **5. Odor** . . . The cleanly odor of "Lysol" disappears after use. **6. Stability** . . . "Lysol" keeps its full strength no matter how long it is kept, or how often it might be left uncorked.

Lysol
Disinfectant

FOR FEMININE HYGIENE

··· PASTE THIS COUPON ON A PENNY POSTCARD! **···**

What Every Woman Should Know
SEND COUPON FOR "LYSOL" BOOKLET
LEHN & FINK PRODUCTS CORP.
Dept. S.S.-404, Bloomfield, N. J., U. S. A.

Send me free booklet "Lysol vs. Germs" which tells the many uses of "Lysol".

*Name*_____

*Address*_____
Copyright, 1940, by Lehn & Fink Products Corp.

Lysol, Lehn & Fink Agency, *Silver Screen*, 1939

"Held in a web of indifference..."

Day after heartbreaking day I was held in an unyielding web . . . a web spun by my husband's indifference. I couldn't reach him any more! Was the fault *mine?* Well . . . thinking you know about feminine hygiene, yet trusting to *now-and-then* care, can make all the difference in married happiness, as my doctor pointed out. He said never to run such careless risks . . . prescribed "Lysol" brand disinfectant for douching—always.

"But I broke through it!"

Oh, the joy of finding Tom's love and close companionship once more! Believe me, I follow *to the letter* my doctor's advice on feminine hygiene . . . always use "Lysol" for douching. I wouldn't be satisfied now with salt, soda or other homemade solutions! Not with "Lysol," a proved *germ-killer* that cleanses so gently yet so thoroughly. It's *easy* to use, too, and *economical*. The very best part is—"Lysol" *really works!*

Many doctors recommend "LYSOL" for Feminine Hygiene...for 6 reasons

Reason No. 5: DEPENDABLE UNIFORMITY . . . Uniform in strength, "Lysol" is made under continued laboratory control—is far more effective than homemade douching solutions.

Note: Douche *thoroughly* with correct "Lysol" solution . . . always!

For Feminine Hygiene use "*Lysol*" *always!*
Brand Disinfectant
REG U S PAT OFF

HOW CAN IT BE TACTFULLY TOLD
to a sensitive young wife?

No other type liquid antiseptic-germicide tested for the douche is so powerful yet safe to tissues

In this modern age, a woman must realize how wise it always is to put ZONITE in her fountain syringe for hygiene (*internal* cleanliness), for her health, charm, after her periods—and *especially* to follow this hygienic practice when she is married. She must realize there's a very common odor which she herself may not detect but is so apparent to people around her.

AND ISN'T IT REASSURING FOR A WIFE TO KNOW THAT NO OTHER TYPE LIQUID ANTISEPTIC-GERMICIDE TESTED FOR THIS PURPOSE IS SO POWERFULLY EFFECTIVE YET SAFE TO TISSUES AS ZONITE.

Truly a Modern Miracle!

Modern women no longer have to use dangerous products, overstrong solutions of which may gradually cause serious damage. Nor will they want to rely on weak homemade solutions—

© 1950 Z.P.C.

none of which have ZONITE's remarkable deodorizing, germ-killing action.

Developed by a famous surgeon and scientist—this ZONITE principle is POWERFULLY EFFECTIVE YET POSITIVELY NON-POISONOUS, NON-IRRITATING. You can use it as directed as often as you want, without the slightest risk of injury.

Gives BOTH Internal and External Hygienic Protection

ZONITE deodorizes not by just "masking"—it actually destroys, dissolves and removes odor-causing waste substances. Use ZONITE and be assured you won't offend. ZONITE has such a soothing effect and promptly helps relieve itching and irritation if present. ZONITE gives daily *external* hygienic protection, too, leaving you with such a refreshed dainty feeling. Buy ZONITE today!

Zonite
FOR NEWER
feminine hygiene

*Offer good only in the U. S.

FREE! NEW!

For amazing enlightening NEW Booklet containing frank discussion of intimate physical facts, recently published—mail this coupon to Zonite Products Corp., Dept. MR-60, 100 Park Avenue, New York 17, N. Y.*

Name_____

Address_____

City_____ State_____

Lux, J. Walter Thompson Agency, *Redbook*, 1942

Avoid Offending—
LUX undies daily

WE ALL PERSPIRE up to 2 or 3 pints a day, scientists say. Undies absorb the odor. You don't notice it, but others do.

Play safe — Lux underthings after ry wearing. New, quick Lux whisks y perspiration odor fast, yet safely.

Undies new-looking longer!

Luxing keeps undies like new much r, too. Avoid harsh y soaps—cake-soap . New, quick Lux is nything safe in water.

cious foundations by em often, too. Gentle he rubber and fabric.

UX is thrifty—
one box will do!

New
Quick
LUX

LUX

BEAUTIFUL BUT DUMB

SHE HAS NEVER LEARNED THE FIRST RULE OF
LASTING CHARM

A *Long-Lasting* Deodorant

People on-the-go use

ODO·RO·NO

Because you are the very
air he breathes...

Early in the last century Edna
Murphy's father, a surgeon, created
a liquid anti-perspirant to keep his
hands sweat-free during operations.

Edna tried his liquid on her armpits,
found it eradicated wetness and
odour, and decided to try and
market the miracle product.

She named it Odorono (Odour?
Oh No!)

Initial reaction was discouraging.

Her door-to-door salesmen were
finding little success, and retailers
weren't interested; any orders they
took were returned unsold.

In 1910, a Victorian attitude still
prevailed in America, and nobody
talked about perspiration or any
other bodily functions in public.

Most people's solution to body odour was to wash, and then overwhelm any smells that developed, particularly on warm days, with perfume.

If you were concerned about sweat marks on your clothing, you placed cotton or rubber pads around the armpit to protect the fabric from perspiration marks.

The breakthrough for Odorono came at the Atlantic City Exposition of 1912, during the particularly hot summer.

Odorono's booth became increasingly popular as sweat poured from visitors' underarms, and word quickly spread nationally about the wonder brand.

Murphy decided to hire J. Walter Thompson as her advertising agency, and their first advertisement pointed out that Odorono had been developed by a doctor, presenting excessive perspiration as a medical ailment cured by the new product.

Friends ARE TOO TIMID TO TELL HER . . .
and she *permits*
a condition ABHORRENT to everyone

?

ENTRUST YOUR *Charm* TO NOTHING LESS SURE THAN ODO·RO·NO

You'd blush with humiliation . . . you'd be shamed to tears if you knew how needlessly you offend other people.

And you *do* offend them—you *do* lose friends—when you permit perspiration to go unchecked. For your own underarm odor . . . so unbearable to others . . . is seldom perceptible to you. Rarely do you know your own offense.

Your underarms may even *seem* dry, but perspiration moisture in the confined armpits quickly forms an acid that ruins dresses and turns friends against you. Even frequent bathing is never enough.

If you care at all what other people think, you'll insist on a deodorant that's trustworthy and sure. You *can* trust Odorono . . . a physician's formula . . . to protect you so completely that your mind is always free of all fear of offending.

ODO·RO·NO is Sure

And by checking, safely and completely, all underarm moisture, it saves your dresses from ruinous stains. Actually it saves its cost fifty times a year, and all year long it protects you from loss of respect, loss of friends and social defeat.

Determine to get Odorono today. For quick, convenient use choose Instant Odorono. Use it daily or every other day for complete, continuous protection. For longest protection or special need, choose Odorono Regular and use it faithfully twice a week. Both Odoronos have the original sanitary applicator. Both come in 35c and 60c sizes.

ODO·RO·NO
Never Fails You

● The Odorono original sanitary applicator is easier and more convenient to use. It holds just enough liquid at a time, and it is washable, too.

Millions of women . . . in 73 countries all over the world . . . trust *their* charm only to Odorono's safe and sure protection. Odorono *is* sure and certain.

It's approved by Good Housekeeping, and used by doctors and nurses everywhere. Let no one think *you* undainty . . . be faithful to Odorono.

RUTH MILLER, THE ODORONO CO., Inc.
Dept.6-Q4, 191 Hudson St., New York City
(In Canada, address P.O. Box 2320, Montreal)
I enclose 10c for a special introductory bottle of Odorono with original sanitary applicator. (Check the type you wish to try) . . .
☐ Instant Odorono   ☐ Odorono Regular

Name...

Address...

Odo-ro-no, J Walter Thompson Agency, *Photoplay*, 1934

Society simply *won't* stand for Indelicate Women

As quick as a wink, a few sprinkles of Amolin will guard your freshness and wholesomeness all day long!

AS SOON as you step from your bath, while the delicious glow of the towel is still upon you, throw under your arms a light coating of Amolin.

For Amolin is a delicate deodorizer *sans reproche*. It does not cover up odors but absorbs them as they arise all day long! It is the clean, fastidious way of disbarring from society the slightest trace of offensive personal odor.

Without smothering the natural function of the pores, Amolin actually counteracts the odors as soon as they are formed. And it protects, rather than harms, your silken underclothes.

This Personal Deodorant has many uses

There are many uses of this wonderful, scientific powder! Use it after your bath, sprinkle it, if you wish, into your lingerie as you dress, put it in your slippers—you can be free with its use for it is harmless and not at all costly! It is pleasant to smell—but its odor is gone as soon as it touches you! For Amolin does not cover up one odor with another, but neutralizes all personal odors as they arise!

So, go dancing, go shopping, swing your arms in golf or tennis, do a day's work in a hot office, for Amolin used after your bath or sprinkled in your underclothes will protect you all day long!

1 *Always use Amolin under the arms when dressing for any social activity*

2 *The most fastidious women use Amolin after the bath all over the body*

3 *Amolin protects delicate lingerie and keeps elastic girdles fresh and sweet*

Norwich
MAKERS OF UNGUENTINE

Amolin

Sold in two sizes—30¢ and 60¢

THE NORWICH PHARMACAL CO., Dept. D-79
Norwich, N. Y.
or 193 Spadina Ave., Toronto

Enclosed is 10¢. Please send me the generous test can of Amolin.

Name...

Address.......................................

Amolin, Young & Rubicam Agency, *Photoplay*, 1929

Initially sales were developing well, but then stalled.

The agency discovered that although the product was now well-known, two thirds of women felt they had no need for it.

They switched advertising strategy to convince women that visible sweating was a social embarrassment, and that although nobody would mention it, people would talk behind your back about the offensiveness of your body odour.

It didn't take long for competitors to mimic Odorono's 'whisper' campaigns to scare women into buying anti-sweat products.

By 1937, a Mum deodorant advertisement stated: 'There are so many pretty women out there who never seem to sense the real reason for their aloneness. In this smart modern age, it's against the code for a girl (or a man either) to carry the repellent odour of underarm perspiration on clothing and person. It's a fault which never fails to carry its own punishment – unpopularity.'

The reference to men was the first tentative step to begin selling antiperspirants to males, as manufacturers grasped that 50% of the market was being left untapped.

Men took time to overcome the notion that using a deodorant was sissified, but advertisements preyed on their insecurities about losing their jobs if their body odour was disagreable, and that unprofessional grooming could ruin their careers.

Soon, Mum and Odorono and the other brands were suggesting on the bottom of their ads 'Women, it's time to stop letting your men be smelly. When you buy one, buy two.'

Today, the deodorant business has grown from a pre-surgery aid for Dr Murphy, to a $20 billion US industry.

Hips aren't your big problem, Honey!

YOU CAN TAKE your hips right off your mind, Angel. For no one finds fault with your *figure!*

But you'd be smart to exercise a little more care about personal charm. Being streamlined, you know, won't protect you against *underarm odor.* Or lessen the offense when others find you guilty.

So keep right on trusting your bath—for *past* perspiration. But put your trust in dependable Mum to prevent risk of *future* underarm odor.

Creamy, snowy-white Mum smooths on in 30 seconds. Keeps you fresh and free from underarm odor all day or evening. Helps you stay nice to be near.

Mum is gentle—is harmless to skin and fabrics. Won't dry out in the jar or form irritating crystals. So why take chances with your charm when you can be *sure* with Mum? Ask for a jar of it today.

• • •

For Sanitary Napkins—*Mum is gentle, safe, dependable…ideal for this use, too.*

Product of Bristol-Myers

Mum
TAKES THE ODOR OUT OF PERSPIRATION

"THERE'S ONE GIRL I'LL NEVER DANCE WITH AGAIN!"

But there's plenty of dates and partners for the girl who uses MUM

"NEVER again for me, Tom! Janet's a peach of a girl and a swell dancer, but some things get a man down. Too bad somebody doesn't tip her off. Other girls know how to avoid underarm odor."

Other girls! Janet thinks about them, too. Wonders why other girls have partners dance after dance—why men so often dance with her just *once.* But no *man*—or girl—likes to come straight out and say, "*Janet, you need Mum.*"

It's so easy to offend—and never know it! That's why, nowadays, no wise girl trusts a bath alone to keep her fresh all evening long. Baths remove *past* perspi-

ration, but Mum prevents odor *to come.* Mum is the quick, pleasant, unfailing way to safeguard your charm for men!

MUM SAVES TIME! A pat under this arm, under that—in 30 seconds you're *done!*

MUM IS SAFE! Even after underarm shaving, Mum is soothing to your skin. Mum is harmless to fabrics—convenient to use *after* you're dressed!

MUM IS SURE! Without stopping perspiration, Mum stops odor for a full day or evening. Remember, men avoid girls who offend! Get Mum at your druggist's today—be sure *you're* always sweet!

AFTER-BATH FRESHNESS SOON FADES WITHOUT MUM

I USED TO THINK A BATH WAS ENOUGH. GLAD I LEARNED ABOUT MUM!

TO HERSELF: I'VE NEVER HAD SUCH A WHIRL! I'VE DANCED ALL EVENING BUT MUM STILL KEEPS ME SWEET!

For Sanitary Napkins— *Mum leads all deodorants for use on napkins, too. Women know it's safe, sure. Use Mum this way.*

Mum
TAKES THE ODOR OUT OF PERSPIRATION

Mum, Doherty, Clifford & Sheffield Agency, *Screenland*, November 1945
Mum, Doherty, Clifford & Sheffield Agency, *Hollywood*, January 1938

He said "Good Night" but he meant "Goodbye"

because of that!

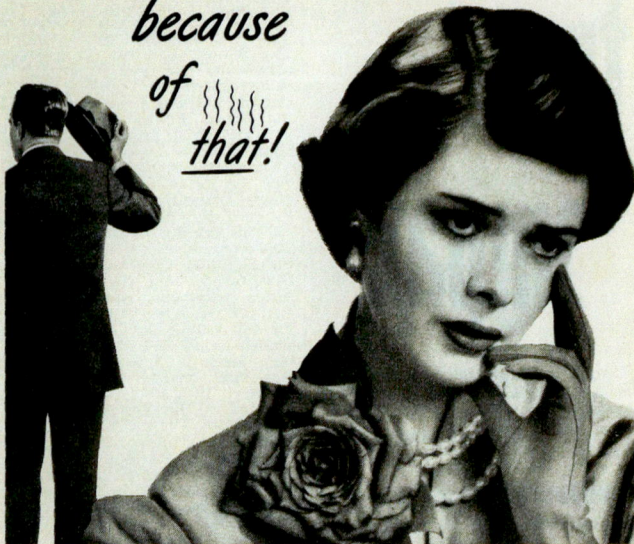

Don't let DEODORANT FAILURE rob you of popularity...

Use *Heed* ® new spray deodorant...stops perspiration

ONE SPRAY IS WORTH A DOZEN DABS

No wonder women everywhere are changing to new, spray-on HEED in the flexible squeeze bottle. HEED stops perspiration...prevents underarm odor all the live-long day. HEED is so easy, so dainty to use—no more messy fingers. No other type deodorant, no cream or old-fashioned liquid gives such long-lasting protection so quickly. So don't take chances with short-time deodorants...use HEED. At all cosmetic counters, 49¢. Lasts many months!

Never be **Heed·less** *and you'll always be safe!*

Heed, *Radio and Television Mirror,* 1950

because *you* are the very air he breathes...

Nothing matters but you two. Your world is all wrapped up in this one momentous moment. Don't let *anything* spoil it. Double check your charm every day with VETO ...the deodorant that drives away odor...dries away perspiration worries. (Remember, if you're nice-to-be-next-to...next to *nothing* is impossible!)

VETO is for you in more ways than one   Cream   Spray   Stick   Aerosol Mist

Veto deodorant

One touch of VETO dries away perspiration worries!

133

Veto, Norman, Craig & Kummel Agency, 1957

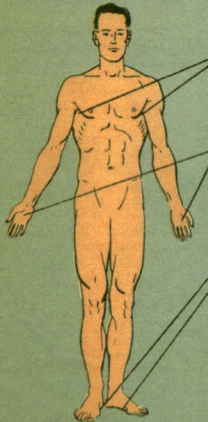

Lifebuoy, Ruthrauff & Ryan Agency, *This Week*, 1940

Beeeeeee-Ohhhhhh

In the 1930s Lifebuoy Soap launched advertisements to alert the public about 'B.O.', laying claim to creating widespread anxiety about body odour.

Their ubiquitous radio commercials 'Lifebuoy really stops...' – cue a sinister-sounding foghorn and a deep voice calling 'Beeeeeee-Ohhhhhh!' – became a siren call to Americans to address the issue of their personal hygiene.

Lifebuoy was one of the earliest soap brands, and was launched in England in 1895 by Lever Brothers, in competition with Procter & Gamble's Ivory soap.

Its powerful carbolic fragrance was reassuring to consumers, who quickly learnt from Lifebuoy advertising to be concerned that you may be giving offence to anyone standing near them.

Lifebuoy, Ruthrauff & Ryan Agency, *Good Housekeeping*, 1937

Lifebuoy promoted the notion that a daily bath or shower with the soap would impact favourably on your success in business and in your social life.

The brand could be trusted to eliminate not only germs, dirt and perspiration, but its 'Purifying Ingredient' could rid your entire body of any residual freshness concerns.

It became accepted that you were being considerate to others to regularly use Lifebuoy, and that to ignore its benefits could render you unpopular.

Each package of Lifebuoy emphasised the bold phrase 'Knocks out B.O.', and although it carried a robustly medicinal, creosote-like odour, advertisements pointed out this quickly disappeared, leaving you smelling appealingly fresh.

In 1987 Lifebuoy became part of the giant Unilever conglomerate of household and food products, but due to regulation by the European Union, it could no longer contain carbolic for EU markets because it was deemed potentially toxic.

This has not hindered the product still being manufactured and distributed, and it remains the leading soap brand in India and much of Southern Asia.

In truth, although the advertising for products like Lifebuoy, Odorono, and Mum may have heartlessly preyed on people's insecurities, was it not essentially also a public benefit?

Imagine how very unpleasant travelling in crowded buses or underground transport would be, before it became customary for most people to bathe and deodorise daily.

Marketers of these products could justifiably claim that their harsh tactics helped modern mankind evolve more quickly, and to learn in just two decades to accept the importance of personal hygiene.

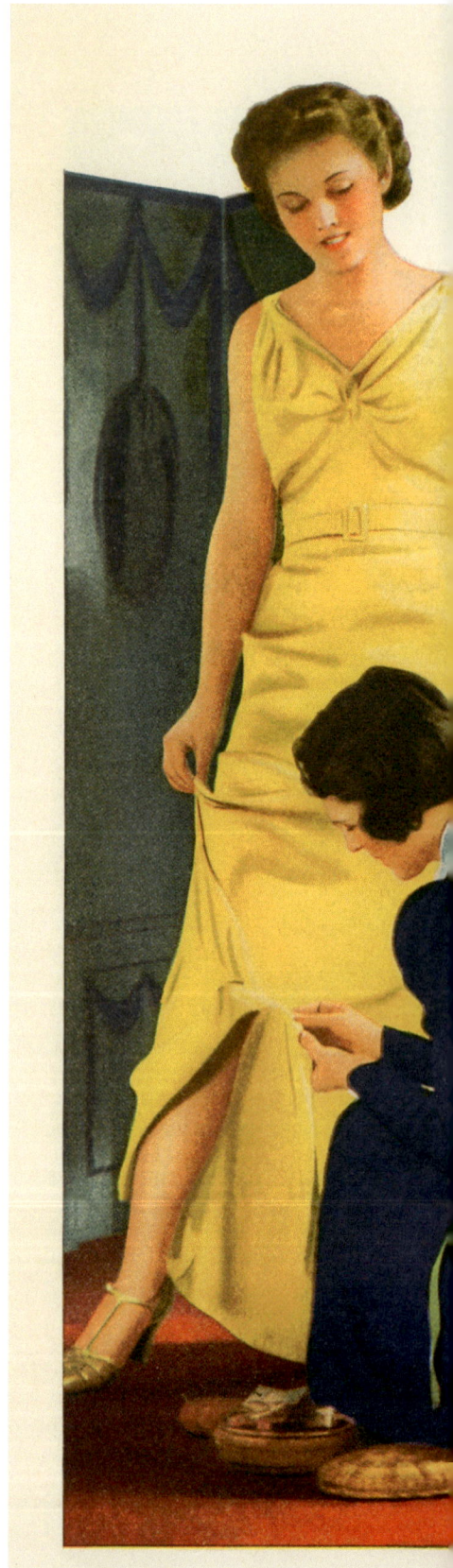

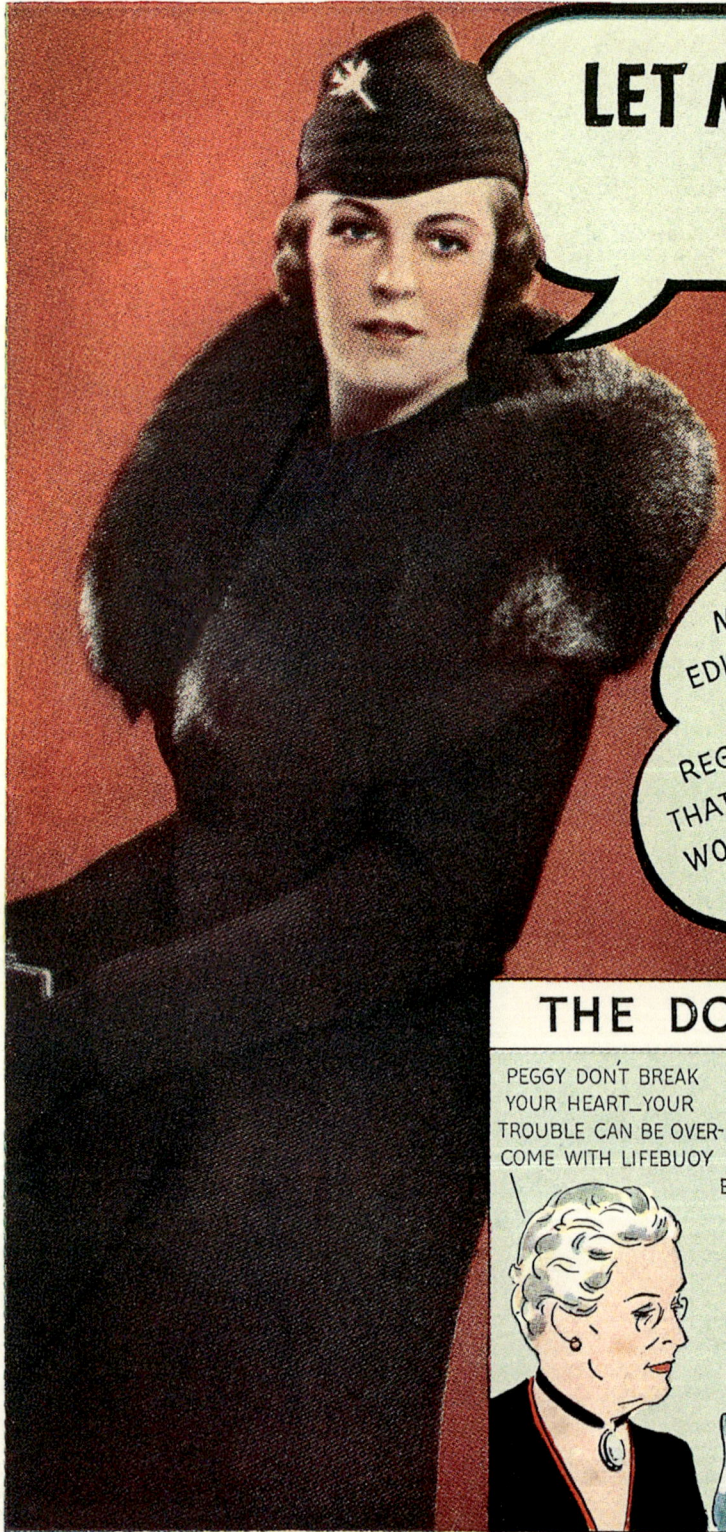

NE WEALTHY DEBUTANTE
A HUSBAND

Editor of New York Post

GORGEOUS LOOKING DEB IF THERE
 ONE...AND HER GOWN! STRAIGHT
RUE DE LA PAIX...IF ANY GIRL WAS
ED IN STYLE IT WAS PEGGY...

BUT DESPITE HER DAD'S MONEY AND HER
OWN OBVIOUS CHARM, SHE WAS A COMPLETE
FLOP...HER PERSONAL MAID KNEW THE
REASON BUT ONLY HER GRANDMOTHER
HAD THE COURAGE TO TELL HER

COVERED PEGGY'S LAST PARTY..SINCE SHE'S
ECOME A REGULAR LIFEBUOY USER, SHE'S THE
OST RUSHED DEB OF THE SEASON! SHE'S EN-
GED TO A DISTINGUISHED YOUNG DIPLOMAT, AND
AVES SHORTLY FOR EUROPE..GOOD LUCK, PEGGY!

FOR GLAMOROUS SKIN—

CLEANSE your face *regularly* with
thrilling Lifebuoy lather. It
freshens tired skin—flatters skin
already lovely . . . It cleanses thoroughly, gently! "Patch" tests on
the skins of hundreds of women
show Life-
buoy is over
20% milder
than many
so-called
"beauty"
and "baby
soaps."

LIFEBUOY
HEALTH SOAP

Approved by
Good Housekeeping Bureau

UNTIL ....

Lifebuoy, Ruthrauff & Ryan Agency, *Puck*, 1947

AN ADVERTISEMENT FOR LEVER BROTHERS CO.

YOU 5,000,000 WOMEN WHO WANT TO GET MARRIED:

How's Your Breath Today?

5,000,000 young women become of marriageable age this year... How many of them, we wonder, will make the grade?

One thing is certain; they can't expect to attract and hold men if they have halitosis (unpleasant breath). It nullifies every other charm.

Everyone is likely to have halitosis at one time or another. When that time comes, you won't realize it, because halitosis does not announce itself to its victim.

Why risk offending, when Listerine will put you on the safe side?

Simply rinse the mouth with it. Every morning and every night, and between times before meeting others. Listerine instantly halts fermentation, the cause of 90% of mouth odors; then gets rid of the odors themselves. The breath becomes sweet and agreeable.

USE LISTERINE BEFORE ALL SOCIAL ENGAGEMENTS

Listerine, Lambert & Feasley Agency, *Photoplay*, 1934

Do they say it of you? Maybe...

Joseph Lister created Listerine in 1879 but found it hard to work out exactly what it was good for.

He began by trying to market it as a surgical antiseptic, and then a household antiseptic.

It was also promoted it as a remedy for gonorrhoea, for athlete's foot, as a cure for the common cold, a dandruff treatment, an aftershave, even a floor cleaner.

It took 40 years, but by the 1920s Listerine had finally found its place in the market – oral hygiene.

It utilised the classic advertising tool – 'invent a problem; provide the cure'.

Faced with the task of persuading people to use mouthwash, at a time when people were not particularly interested in taking care of their breath, Listerine decided they should appeal to people's insecurities.

They stumbled on the word halitosis, an antiquated Latin clinical term for bad breath.

Of course the public were not familiar with it, until a marketing campaign ran by Listerine in the 1920s.

Fueling people's fears that they may suffer from this serious-sounding problem, within a decade using mouthwash went from something that nobody did, to becoming a daily routine for Americans believing themselves to possibly be plagued with an unpleasant medical condition.

Other companies were awestruck by Listerine's marketing initiative, and tried to imitate it by producing any number of spurious problems they could help you with; suddenly the public learned to be anxious about bromodosis – you may have un-pleasantly smelly feet, yet be unaware that others are gossiping about it.

You can lose him in a minute!

IT has happened to thousands of girls . . . it can happen to you.

One little moment's carelessness and he will be through with you *that quick!* You will probably ask yourself over and over again, "Why? Why? Why?"

How About You?

Never let halitosis (unpleasant breath) nullify your other charms. Never, never omit Listerine Antiseptic before any date where you want to be at your best.

Listerine Antiseptic is the *extra-careful* precaution against offending because it freshens and sweetens the breath . . . helps keep it that way, too . . . not for seconds . . . not for minutes . . . but for hours usually. Get in the habit of using Listerine Antiseptic night and morning, and, we repeat, always before any date.

While some cases of halitosis are of systemic origin, most cases, say some authorities, are due to the bacterial fermentation of tiny food particles clinging to mouth surfaces. Listerine Antiseptic quickly halts such fermentation, then overcomes the odors fermentation causes. Lambert Pharmacal Co., *St. Louis, Mo.*

LISTERINE ANTISEPTIC . . . the *extra-careful* precaution against Bad Breath

Week-ending? Always take Listerine Antiseptic along. It's mighty comforting to have a good antiseptic handy in case of minor cuts, scratches and abrasions requiring germicidal first-aid.

Listerine, Lambert & Feasley Agency, *Radio and Television Mirror*, 1950

"If you want the truth—

—go to a child." And the old saying is certainly true, isn't it?

Here was the case of a young woman who, in spite of her personal charm and beauty, never seemed to hold men friends.

For a long, long time she searched her mind for the reason. It was a tragic puzzle in her life.

Then one day her little niece told her.

* * *

You, yourself, rarely know when you have halitosis (unpleasant breath). That's the insidious thing about it. And even your closest friends won't tell you.

Sometimes, of course, halitosis comes from some deep-seated organic disorder that requires professional advice. But usually—and fortunately—halitosis is only a local condition that yields to the regular use of Listerine as a mouth wash and gargle. It is an interesting thing that this well-known antiseptic that has been in use for years for surgical dressings, possesses these unusual properties as a breath deodorant. It puts you on the safe and polite side

Listerine halts food fermentation in the mouth and leaves the breath sweet, fresh and clean. The entire mouth feels invigorated.

Get in the habit of using Listerine every morning and night. And between times before social and business engagements. It's the fastidious thing to do. *Lambert Pharmacal Company, St. Louis, Missouri.*

For HALITOSIS use LISTERINE

This school of marketing even had a name: the Halitosis Appeal.

Listerine were keen to point out that 'you could lose your man in a minute' if you didn't guard against bad breath.[186]

They also recommended that you ask a child to tell you the truth about your breath – they could be relied upon for a straightforward response, as they wouldn't be aware that they were possibly being rude or hurtful.

And so, Listerine advertising featured a friendless woman who was shown asking her baby niece for a critique of her breath.

Chlorodent toothpaste was happy to suggest that women were spider-like creatures, ready to catch your man in their web, if you weren't careful about your 'morning mouth'.[196]

The most effective of the mouth odour campaigns was undoubtedly Listerine's whisper advertising.

Targeting both men and women, they detailed the variety of comments others may be saying behind your back.

'You would never invite her twice'

'I wish I had the courage to tell her'

'One dance is enough with her'

'She's a nice girl, but…'

'His wife ought to tell him'

'Such a nice fellow otherwise'

Preying on insecurities in this way became the cornerstone of much advertising of the era, and it was a route favoured by brands over the following decades, subtler and less direct, but no less effective.

Today, toothpastes and mouthwashes suggest their brands will make your mouth 'fresh and tingly' rather than suggesting your breath is so unpleasant it would startle a horse.

They say it about her . . .

"THEY NEVER INVITE HER TWICE"

"SHE'S GOT 'IT'—THE WRONG KIND"

"SHE'S A NICE GIRL, BUT—"

"HAS SHE ALWAYS BEEN THAT WAY?"

"ONE DANCE IS ENOUGH—WITH HER"

"I DON'T BLAME HIM FOR BREAKING THE ENGAGEMENT"

"I WISH I HAD THE COURAGE TO TELL HER"

"SHE SIMPLY CANNOT HOLD ON TO A FELLOW"

. . . they may say it about you

WHAT a pity it is that so many otherwise fastidious men and women give no thought to keeping their breath beyond reproach.

The case of this attractive Boston girl is typical. Her charm is undeniable. Her clothes are the envy of less fortunate women. Actually, she's one girl in a thousand. Yet her women friends, if they invite her to parties at all, invite her out of courtesy. As for men, they call once and that is the end of it. Halitosis (unpleasant breath) is too high a hurdle for sensitive people.

You yourself cannot be sure that at this very moment you are free of halitosis. The damnable thing about this condition is that while obvious to others, the victim herself is seldom aware of it. So many every day conditions are responsible for halitosis that few people escape it entirely—food fermentation in the mouth, defective or decaying teeth, pyorrhea, catarrh, or other mild infections of the mouth, nose, and throat. Also stomach derangements caused by excesses of eating or drinking.

The swift, certain way to put your breath beyond suspicion is to rinse your mouth with full strength Listerine, the safe antiseptic, morning and night, and between times before meeting others. Keep a bottle handy at home and office for this purpose.

Being a safe but active germicide,* full strength Listerine checks decomposition and infection which cause odors. Then, being a powerful deodorant, overcomes the odors themselves.

Do not expect ordinary antiseptics, lacking Listerine's germicidal potency, to be effective against this humiliating condition. Lambert Pharmacal Company, St. Louis, Mo., U. S. A.

*Full strength Listerine kills 200,000,000 Staphylococcus Aureus (pus) and Bacillus Typhosus (typhoid) germs in 15 seconds—fastest time science has accurately recorded—twenty times faster than is required by the U. S. Government to qualify as a germicide.

Listerine *ends* halitosis

In 1925, Listerine coined the
phrase 'Often a bridesmaid…
never a bride' in their promotion.

This expression has been in
common usage ever since, with
few remembering its derivation –
Listerine advertising.

Often a bridesmaid...

never a bride!

Most of the girls of her set were married . . . but not Eleanor. It was beginning to look, too, as if she never would be. True, men were attracted to her, but their interest quickly turned to indifference. Poor girl! She hadn't the remotest idea why they dropped her so quickly . . . and even her best friend wouldn't tell her.

**No tooth paste kills germs
like this . . . instantly**

Listerine Antiseptic does for you what no tooth paste does. Listerine instantly kills germs, by millions—stops bad breath (halitosis) instantly, and usually for hours on end.

Far and away the most common cause of bad breath is germs. You see, germs cause fermentation of proteins, which are always present in the mouth. *And research shows that your breath stays sweeter longer, the more you reduce germs in the mouth.*

Tooth paste with the aid of a tooth brush is an effective method of oral hygiene. But no tooth paste gives you the proven Listerine Antiseptic method—banishing bad breath with super-efficient germ-killing action.

**Listerine Antiseptic clinically proved
four times better than tooth paste**

Is it any wonder Listerine Antiseptic in recent clinical tests averaged at least four times more effective in stopping bad breath odors than the chlorophyll products or tooth pastes it was tested against? Every night . . . before every date, make it a habit to use Listerine, the most widely used antiseptic in the world.

LISTERINE ANTISEPTIC STOPS BAD BREATH
...4 TIMES BETTER THAN ANY TOOTH PASTE

Listerine, Lambert & Feasley Agency, *Modern Screen*, 1954

You can mask the odor of "morning mouth" for a while with any toothpaste. But Chlorodent actually gets rid of it

No Halloween mask scares off a man

AS MUCH AS "MORNING MOUTH"

We'll confess—if you will.

You know when you wake up your breath is not as fresh as it might be. That stale and furry taste is a sure sign of bad breath.

And we know simply using Chlorodent, our *chlorophyll-plus* toothpaste, won't get you married within a week . . . or make your husband shower you with orchids!

But we do say Chlorodent gets rid of "morning mouth." Its generous helping of chlorophyll ends bad breath for hour after hour. And here's the "plus", Chlorodent brightens the teeth

measurably better than any other leading toothpaste formula.

This we guarantee—or Lever Brothers Co. will return your money. Isn't that reason enough for buying Chlorodent *today?*

P.S.—And all this goes for Chlorodent Tooth Powder, too.

"Anti-enzyme," too, for continuing decay protection

University dentists found that just one brushing with Chlorodent keeps "enzyme" decay acids below the danger point for 9 out of 10 people for hours.

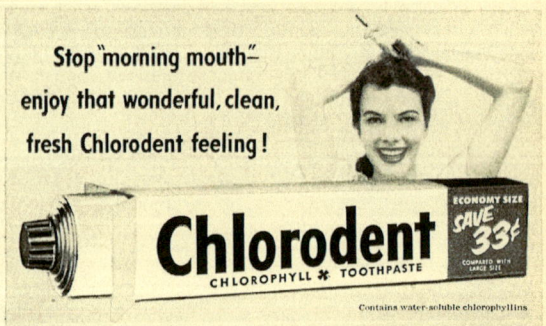

Stop "morning mouth"— enjoy that wonderful, clean, fresh Chlorodent feeling!

Chlorodent
CHLOROPHYLL ✻ TOOTHPASTE

ECONOMY SIZE SAVE 33¢ COMPARED WITH LARGE SIZE

Contains water-soluble chlorophyllins

2 LIFE October 26, 1953 LIFE is published weekly by TIME Inc., 540 N. Michigan Ave., Chicago 11, Ill. Printed in U. S. A. Entered as second-class matter November 16, 1936 at the Postoffice at Chicago, Ill. under the act of March 3, 1879. Authorized by Post Office Department, Ottawa, Canada, as second-class matter. Subscriptions $6.75 a year in U. S. A.; $7.25 in Canada. Volume 35 Number 17

Chlordent, J. Walter Thompson Agency, 1953

This 1953 advertisement was produced by the J. Walter Thompson agency. They hired leading photographer Saul Leiter for the shoot, and he needed a pumpkin big enough to fit over the model's head.

Failing to find one large enough in the fruit and vegetable markets of New York, in desperation a JWT account executive was despatched, at midnight, to upper Connecticut.

Armed with a torch and a tape measure, he searched through various farmyards until he found the perfect pumpkin.

Chlorodent made the most of its chlorophyll ingredient.

This was the basis for their claim that the product would rid you of your 'morning breath' that could linger all day.

Often, other benefits such as dental hygiene and cleanliness were relegated to the end of the advertising copy, as the fear of halitosis became the paramount reason for selecting your toothpaste.

No wife wants her husband to carry the memory of her morning breath to work with him.
The attractive women he meets during the day don't have it

There's another woman waiting for every man — AND SHE'S TOO SMART TO HAVE "MORNING MOUTH"

We're not saying that if wives simply use Chlorodent their husbands will never look at a pretty girl.

But we do know if you use Chlorodent, your good-bye kiss works for, not against you. For Chlorodent really gets rid of that stale, furry "morning mouth." Your own clean, fresh taste tells you your breath is sweet—even hours later.

The secret is *chlorophyll-plus*. You see, Chlorodent has a big, generous helping of chlorophyll, *plus* a patented cleaning agent. Chlorodent is so effective it *brightens teeth measurably better than any other toothpaste formula, bar none*.

Brighter teeth. A cleaner mouth. An inviting breath. All this we guarantee—or Lever Brothers Company will return your money. Isn't that reason enough for buying Chlorodent—today?

P.S. Same *chlorophyll-plus* benefits in Chlorodent Tooth Powder.

"Anti-enzyme," too, for continuing decay protection

University dentists found the special cleansing agents in Chlorodent keep enzyme decay acids below the danger point for 9 out of 10 people for hours —with just one *brushing*.

Stop "morning mouth"—
enjoy that wonderful, clean,
fresh Chlorodent feeling!

Chlorodent
CHLOROPHYLL ❀ TOOTHPASTE

ECONOMY SIZE
SAVE 33¢
COMPARED WITH LARGE SIZE

Contains water-soluble chlorophyllins.

161

Chlordent, J. Walter Thompson Agency, *Life*, 1953

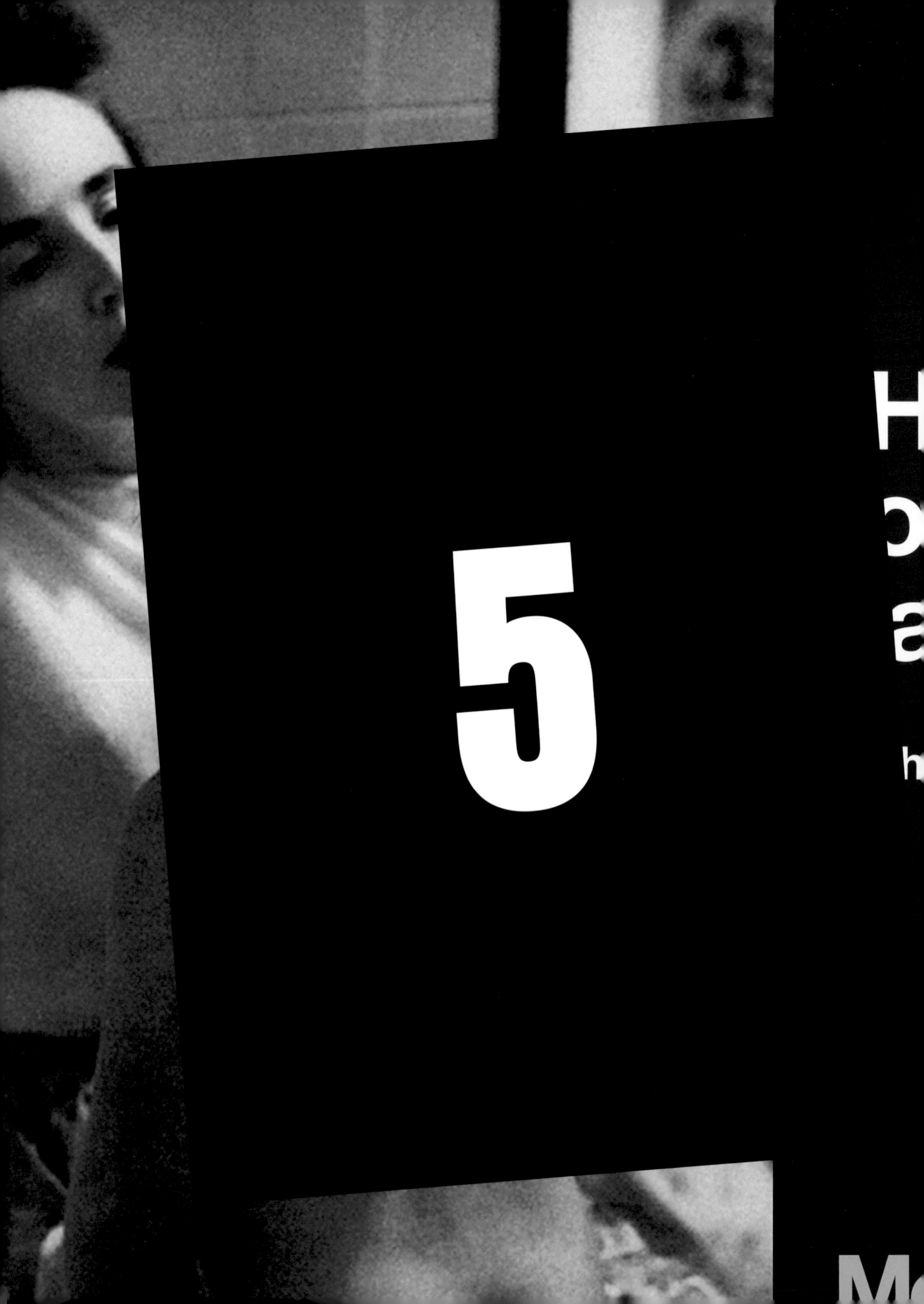

PROZAC NATION....

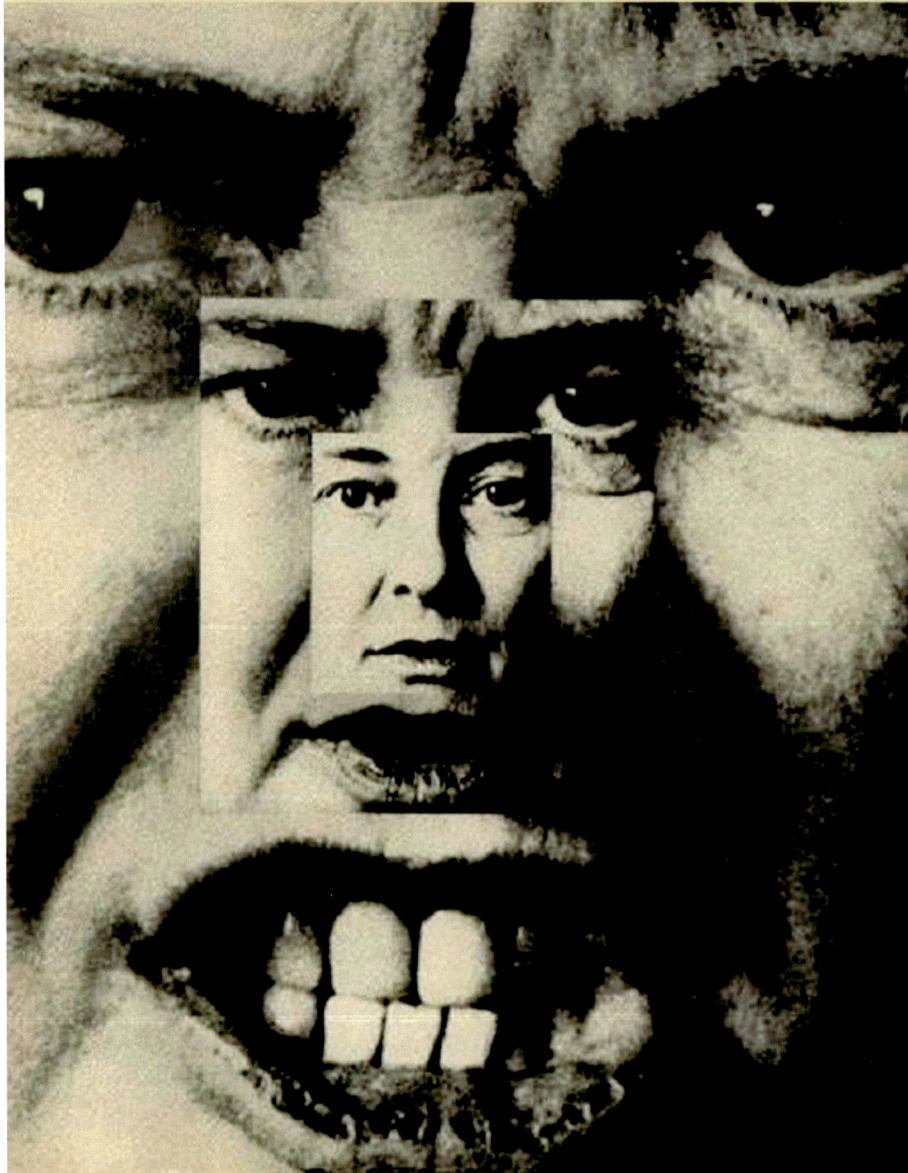

Valium, William Douglas McAdams, Inc. Agency, 1965

Brighten the day the Ritalin way...

In 1971 LY110141 was developed, and this compound was eventually to be branded Prozac. At the time depression was an issue that was rarely discussed, and antidepressants were largely restricted to psychiatric units.

Often, the drugs prescribed by GPs for people who suffered from 'anxiety' and 'nerves' were tranquillisers such as Valium.

They were used routinely to pacify, numb and sedate women, 'helping them behave and appear, as they conventionally should, as a dutiful mother and wife – happily silent and without revolt'.

Eli Lilly, manufacturers of Prozac, originally anticipated a different future for their drug. It was first tested as a treatment for high blood pressure, and then as an anti-obesity agent, but although it produced successful results when tested on animals, it was ineffective in humans.

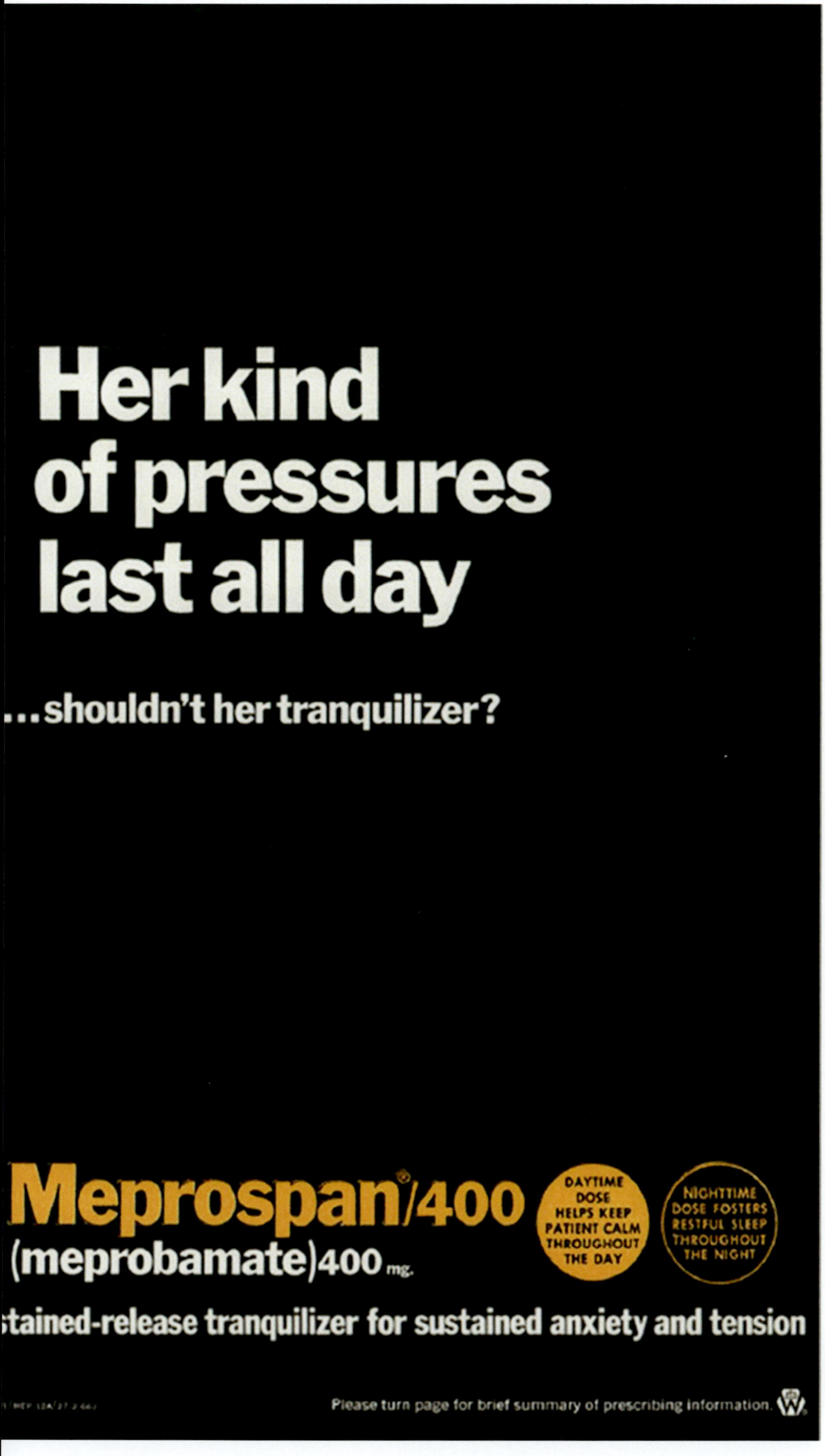

Her kind
of pressures
last all day

...shouldn't her tranquilizer?

Meprospan®/400
(meprobamate)400 mg.

DAYTIME DOSE HELPS KEEP PATIENT CALM THROUGHOUT THE DAY

NIGHTTIME DOSE FOSTERS RESTFUL SLEEP THROUGHOUT THE NIGHT

stained-release tranquilizer for sustained anxiety and tension

Please turn page for brief summary of prescribing information.

Meprospan, Robert & Wilson, Inc Agency, 1957

When Fluoxetine, as Prozac was known before being given its more catchy brand name, was tested on psychiatric patients and those with severe depression, it appeared to have little or no benefit, with some patients actively getting worse.

(Fluoxetine had been assigned to Interbrand, the world's leading identity branding company, and Prozac was created as a name that sounded positive, upbeat, quick and professional.)

Finally, Eli Lilly began analysing it on sufferers from mild depression.

It was trialed on five patients and all of their moods improved significantly.

More testing demonstrated such high levels of benefit, the drug was given Food and Drug Administration approval.

for proved antidepressant effect–
both rapid and prolonged

DEXAMYL® SPANSULE®

brand of dextro amphetamine and amobarbital   **brand of sustained release capsules**

'Dexamyl® has been used successfully for over a decade, and in sustained release form for more than six years. Just one 'Dexamyl' Spansule capsule, taken in the morning, provides daylong therapeutic effect. And mood elevation is usually apparent within 50 to 60 minutes. 'Dexamyl' is of significant value in depressed and verbally inhibited patients. Drayton[1] states, 'Not only does ['Dexamyl'] exert a direct mood effect, so that the shadow of depression is lifted, but it also results in making the patient more approachable and communicative."

1. Drayton. W. Jr. Pennsylvania M.J. 51949

leaders in
psychopharmaceutical research

SMITH KLINE & FRENCH

Dexamyl (Smith, Kline & French), Doremus-Eshlman Co. Agency, 1955

By 1999, Prozac was providing Eli Lilly with more than 25% of its $10 billion revenue.

'Keep calm, take a Prozac' propaganda was quickly embraced into a culture where women's beauty, sexuality and even sanity could be commodified.

It was little coincidence that as a new moral panic developed in the medical community about Valium addiction, Prozac's arrival was trumpeted as an 'easy-to-prescribe one pill, one dose for all, formula'.

National campaigns alerted GPs and the public to the dangers of depression.

This instilled a heightened anxiety about the need for society to medicate, and Prozac was promoted as entirely safe, to be distributed and taken by anyone.

With its vested interest in Prozac, Eli Lilly funded 8 million brochures (Depression: What You Need to Know) and hundreds of thousands of posters, raising concern about this previously undiscussed topic.

IN MILD PSYCHOGENIC DEPRESSIVE STATES . . .
this
IN MINUTES!
. . . WITH
RAPHETAMINE
PHOSPHATE
Brand of Amphetamine Phosphate
CHEERFULNESS
MENTAL ALERTNESS
OPTIMISM
● Smooth, fast acting Raphetamine Phosphate aids in restoring mental alertness, cheerfulness and optimism in mild psychogenic depressive states . . . and in the management of obesity.
With contraindications chiefly limited to hypertensive Cardiac defects of hypersensetivity to ephedrine - like compounds, benefits may be prolonged.
Newly accepted *parenteral* Raphetamine Phosphate can successfully be used in treating barbiturate intoxication because of its immediate action.
Clinical supply of both dosage forms available on request. Write to Medical Service Department, R.J. Strasenburgh Co., Rochester 14. N.Y.
parenteral: Raphetamine Phosphate, parenteral, containing 10mg monobasic acentric amphetamine phosphate per cc 10 sterile aqueous solution is available in 10 cc multidose vials.
tablet: Raphetamine Phosphate tablets containing 5 mg monobasic acentric amphetamine phosphate per tablet are available in bottles of 100, 500 and 1000.
Strasenburgh

for the **overeating** *of the emotionally deprived ...*

The emotionally deprived often find that only the pleasures of the table enliven an otherwise timely and self-centered existence.
'Dexamyl' can help you to relieve—smoothly and subtly—the emotional tension that is often expressed as an almost compulsive desire to nibble and overeat.

Dexamyl* *tablets • elixir • Spansule® capsules*

Each 'Dexamyl' Tablet or teaspoonful (5 cc) of the Elixir contains Dexedrine® Sulfate (dextro-amphetamine sulfate, S.K.F.), 5 mg and amobarbital, ½ gr. Also Available, 'Dexamyl' Spansule (No. 1), slowly releasing the equivalent of two tablets; 'Dexamyl' Spansule (No. 2), slowly releasing the equivalent of three tablets.

Smith, Kline & French Laboratories, Philadelphia (SKF)

*T.M. Reg. U.S. Pat. Off.
†T.M. Reg. U.S. Pat. Off. for sustained release capsules, S.K.F

Dexamyl (Smith, Kline & French), Doremus-Eshlman Co. Agency, 1955

Diagnoses of 'depression' reached epidemic levels and studies suggest that in America, the numbers of the clinically depressed more than doubled between 1991 and 2001.

During the same period in the UK mood enhancement prescriptions rose from 9 million to 24 million a year.

Prozac still remains the most widely used antidepressant in history, taken daily by 54 million people worldwide.

It is also prescribed for a range of ailments such as obsessive-compulsive behaviour, panic attacks, eating disorders and premenstrual dysphoric conditions.

MPH (Methylphenidate) was first approved in the 1950s, and by 1957 Ciba Pharmaceuticals began marketing their product under the brand name Ritalin.

It was utilised to treat chronic fatigue, depression, psychosis, and for ADHD (attention deficit hyperactivity disorder) in children.

Research into the therapeutic values of Ritalin meant that it was also sold for a short period of time as a combination drug, alongside other stimulants and products, improving people's moods whilst maintaining vitality.

Decades later American psychiatrist Leon Eisenberg, the scientific father of ADHD, stated in his last ever interview that: 'ADHD is a prime example of a fictitious disease.'

Ciba also wanted to advertise Ritalin-SR on the basis that children would not have to suffer the 'ridicule over pill-taking' from their peers, as they could avoid having to take the pill during the school day.

The FDA would not allow the company to make this claim.

However, the use of Ritalin to treat ADHD in children increased during the 1970s and early 80s; its use grew alongside an ever-advancing technological and gadget-based culture.

Between 1991 and 1999, Ritalin sales increased by 500%.

In fact, the United States produces and consumes as much as 85% of the world's production of Ritalin.

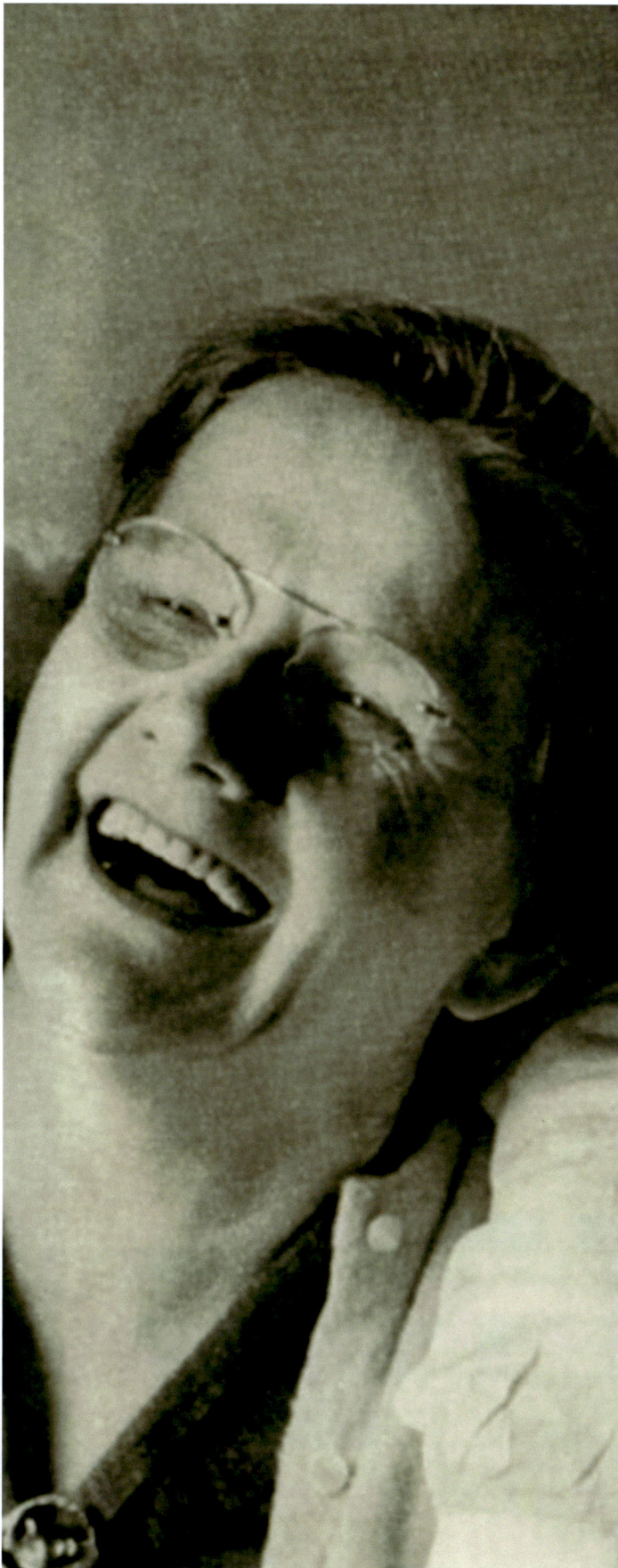

Brighten the day

overcome
depression, fatigue, lethargy

improve
spirits and performance

with

Ritalin
hydrochloride
(methylphenidate hydrochloride USP)

...new mild smooth-acting antide-pressant and stimulant, chemically unrelated to the amphetamines.

• Ritalin brightens outlook and renews vigor—overcomes drug sed-ative effects—often improves behav-ior in the elderly. In most cases Ritalin does not overstimulate, has little or no effect on appetite, blood pressure or pulse rate.

AVERAGE DOSAGE: 10mg b.i.d. or t.i.d.

SUPPLIED: Tablets 5mg (yellow), 10mg (light blue), 20mg (peach colored)

INDICATIONS

· the depressed
· the psychically fatigued
· the apathetic
· the oversedated
· the moody

C I B A SUMMIT, MA

Ritalin, Cortez F. Enloe, Inc. Agency, 1957

if chronic fatigue and mild depression make simple tasks seem this big...

Ritalin gently overcomes mild depression and the fatigue so often associated with it. The drug brightens mood and improves performance, helps restore alertness, enthusiasm, and drive. Patients often report that fatigue and worry seem to vanish; they are able to go all day without getting tired.

Widely cited for its outstanding record of safety, Ritalin is virtually free of the toxic effects of the more potent antidepressants. Its action is usually uncomplicated by excessive stimulation or sudden letdown.

Ritalin is exceptionally well tolerated, even by the elderly.

CONTRAINDICATIONS: Marked anxiety, tension, agitation. Contraindicated in patients with glaucoma and with epilepsy, except to combat lethargy induced by anticonvulsant drugs. WARNINGS: Should not be used for severe depression (exogenous or endogenous) except in the hospital under careful supervision Should not be used to increase mental or physical capacities beyond physiological limits.
PRECAUTIONS: Patients with an element of agitation may react adversely; discontinue therapy if

Ritalin® (methylphenidate CIBA)
relieves chronic fatigue that depresses and mild depression that fatigues

necessary. Use cautiously with vasopressors (*e.g.*, epinephrine, levarterenol, angiotensin amide) and in patients with hypertension.
SIDE EFFECTS: Nervousness, insomnia, anorexia, nausea, dizziness, palpitation, headache, drowsiness, skin rash. Rarely, blood pressure and pulse changes, both up and down, occur. Overt psychotic behavior and psychic dependence in emotionally unstable person's have occurred rarely.

DOSAGE: Administer orally in divided doses 2 or 3 times daily, preferably 30 to 45 minutes before meals. Dosage will depend upon indication and individual response, the average range being 20 to 60 mg daily.
SUPPLIED: Ritalin® hydrochloride (methylphenidate hydrochloride CIBA) *Tablets*, 20 mg (peach), 10 mg (pale green) and 5 mg (pale yellow).
Consult complete product literature before prescribing.
CIBA Pharmaceutical Company, Summit. N. J.

2/3383MB-R2

C I B A

In low doses Ritalin is noted to stimulate appetite suppression, euphoria and heightened alertness – but also nausea in some patients and impairment of voluntary movement.

In high doses it has led not only to exhilaration, but to agitation, confusion, hallucinations, paranoia, seizures, and the sensation of bugs or worms crawling under the skin.

There was little known about serotonin thirty years ago, but now 'serotonin levels' are frequently discussed in relation to happiness and well-being.

According to David Healy, Professor of Psychiatry at Cardiff University and author of *Let Them Eat Prozac*, after having spent a decade researching and testing serotonin on patients suffering from depression, he concluded that there is little evidence to support the theory of a 'chemical imbalance'.

WHEN HE <u>OVERREACTS</u> TO ANY SITUATION

The overreaction of patients to everyday occurrences is often a threat to their well-being. Mebaral reduces restlessness and irritability, and patients become less easily upset. It has the advantages of ". . . extremely low incidence of toxicity . . ." and a *familiar* sedative effect. Mebaral does not produce *sedative daze*. Many physicians prefer the sedative effects of Mebaral to those of phenobarbital.

For daytime sedation—½ grain, ¾ grain and occasionally 1½ grains three or four times daily.

A stumble seems a plunge

MEBARAL®

brand of mephobarbital

SEDATION WITHOUT SEDATIVE DAZE

Bibliography: 1. Brown, W. T., and Smith, J. A.: South. M. J. 46:583, June, 1953. 2. Bevis, R.: Neurology 4:116, Feb., 1954. 3. Baker, A. B.: Personal communication. 4. Jakobson, C.: North Carolina M. J. 8:121, March, 1947. 5. Smith, J. A.: Am. Pract. & Digest Treat. 4:1, July, 1953. 6. Smith, J. A.: J.A.M.A. 152:354, May 30, 1953. 7. Briggs, J. F.: Minnesota Med. 34:1382, Nov., 1951. 8. Briggs, J. F., and Solomon, J.: Dis. Chest 24:65, July, 1953. 9. McCullagh, W. H.: J. Florida M. A. 41:710, March, 1955. 10. Cohen, B., and Myerson, A.: New England J. Med. 227:336, Aug. 27, 1942.

Winthrop
LABORATORIES
New York 18, N.Y.

The growing view is that the concept of human emotions being controlled and affected solely by their serotonin levels is simplified and reductive.

Many specialists claim that such theorising ignores other important factors that contribute to depression.

Interestingly, the Freedom of Information Act revealed several reports which illustrated that in over half of the 47 trials conducted to approve the effectiveness of six leading antidepressants, the drugs failed to significantly outperform placebo sugar pills.

Even when the drugs did outperform the sugar, it was only ever by two points on a 52-point depression rating scale.

According to Anna Moore's 2007 article *Eternal Sunshine*, which explores the history of Prozac, a US survey of drug companies found that between 1995 and 1999, use of Prozac-like drugs for children aged seven to twelve increased by 151%, and those aged under six by 580%.

She goes on to note that in 2004, America's fastest growing sub-group taking antidepressants were, astoundingly, children aged five and under.

Infants were also sedated with Prozac to treat common issues that pre-school children can naturally suffer from, such as 'selective mutism', more commonly known as a child's fear of speaking in social situations.

Between 1992 and 2001, medicating children under the age of eighteen with prescriptions for mood inhibitors in the UK increased tenfold despite NHS warnings about disturbing side effects.

In America such medications, including Prozac, now carry a bold warning that the drugs could increase suicidal behavior in children.

*Tyrant
in the
house?*

Tyrant in the house?

'Thorazine' can control the agitated, belligerent senile

and help the patient to live a composed and useful life

When 'Thorazine' is administered to the agitated senile, there is a marked decrease in his nerve-cracking outbursts of hostility, irritability, abusiveness, incessant talking and 'day and night' pacing or restlessness

On 'Thorazine' therapy, the patient often forms more regular eating and sleeping habits and improves in his personal hygiene. As the patient becomes more stable and cooperative, he is able to live a composed and useful life.

THORAZINE*

one of the funtamental drugs in medicine

Smith Kline & French Laboratories, Philadelphia

People don't like elderly people who aren't cheerful...

The ability to experience happiness can affect the extent to which we can feel our lives to be worthwhile.

'Is feeling old getting you down? Combat Psychic Tension with Valium!'[199]

The elderly became an important new target for medical intervention, aimed at curing them of the grumpiness associated with aging.

Thorazine, Triavil, Loxapac and Butisol grew in popularity with doctors faced with seeking remedies for 'senile agitation'.

The cult status of Valium was even incorporated into the 1966 Rolling Stones hit 'Mother's Little Helper'. 'And though she's not really ill, there's a little yellow pill.'

The FDA first approved
Hoffmann-La Roche's trademark
Valium pill in 1963. After its rise
to fame it became the world's most
widely prescribed answer to anxiety
– and the first drug to reach $1
billion sales.

In 1978, at the height of its
popularity Americans consumed
more than 2 billion units stamped
with the trademark 'V'.

Valium's aggressive marketing
campaign engineered its success.

A 1970s advertisement titled 'Mrs.
Raymond's pupils do a double-take'
revealed Valium as the cure for
middle-aged women who are
debilitated by 'excessive psychic
tension and associated depressive
symptoms accompanying her
menopause'.

The menopause was used to
symbolise the death of a woman's
young and fertile body, but
fortunately the wondrous
'V' was here to save the day.

for prompt control of

senile agitation

THORAZINE*

'Thorazine' can control the agitated, belligerent senile and
help the patient to have an improved and useful life

© Smith Kline & French Laboratories

Thorazine, Doremus-Eshlman Co. Agency, 1957

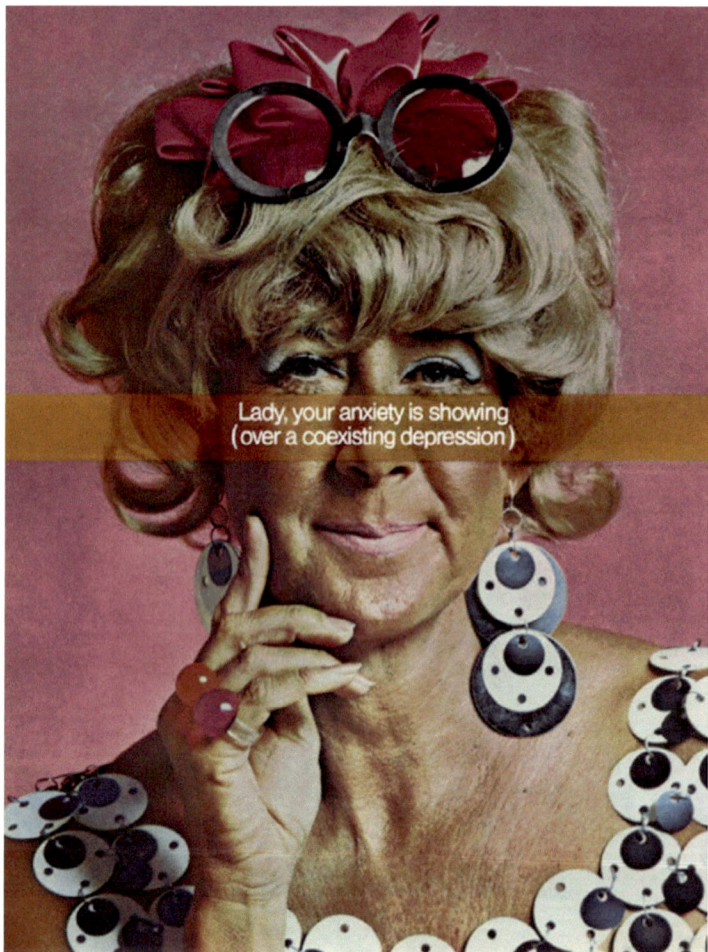

Lady, your anxiety is showing
(over a coexisting depression)

On the visible level, this middle-aged patient dresses to look too young, exhibits a tense, continuous smile, and may have bitten nails or overplucked eyebrows. Symptoms of anxiety are hard to miss. What doesn't show as clearly is the coexisting depression that often complicates treatment.

TRIAVIL offers effective tranquilizer-antidepressant therapy. TRIAVIL provides perphenazine to help allay anxiety and amitriptyline HCl to lift depressive mood and relieve the functional somatic complaints often encountered in patients of this age group.

FOR MODERATE
TO SEVERE ANXIETY **TRIAVIL** containing perphenazine and amitriptyline HCl
WITH DEPRESSION
TRANQUILIZER-ANTIDEPRESSANT

Patients who have received MAO inhibitors within two weeks should not receive TRIAVIL. Those on TRIAVIL should be warned that response to alcohol may be potentiated. The drug may impair alertness in some patients; operation of automobiles and other activities made hazardous by diminished alertness should be avoided. Contraindicated in glaucoma, in patients expected to experience problems of urinary retention, in CNS depression from drugs, and in bone marrow depression. Should not be given with guanethidine or similarly acting compounds. Not recommended in pregnancy. Since the possibility of suicide is inherent in any serious depressive illness, close supervision of patients is essential until you are satisfied that significant remission has taken place.

For additional prescribing information, please see following page.

Sadly, as Woody Allen's 1977 movie *Annie Hall* illustrated, it may leave any woman addicted, and crawling across the floor like Diane Keaton searching for her Valium.

In March 1954 the FDA approved the drug Thorazine.[219/222] It was considered the first form of psychiatric medication that could be taken orally.

The controversial advertisements which documented this new wave of medicines began the radicalisation of mental health treatments.

In some ways they heralded a medical revolution.

The marketing was pivotal in changing the way people thought about treatment for the elderly; medication not aimed at prolonging their lives, or easing their discomfort – but suggesting it would simply make grumpy old people more bearable to have around.

Researchers in France who developed Thorazine thought it could potentially be used to sedate patients during surgery, but later discovered that it produced 'a medicinal lobotomy'.

McNeil Laboratories marketed their
compound as Butisol Sodium,
initially administered to schizo-
phrenics, but subsequently
attracting more widespread use
by middle-aged women.

The advertising catchily claimed:

'Mabel is unstable… It's "that time
in her life". To see her through the
menopause, there's gentle "daytime
sedation" in Butisol Sodium.'

The relationship drawn between
women's menopause and mental
illness was a disturbing one,
considering it an ailment rather a
natural side effect of growing older.

Similarly, Loxapac was an anti-psychotic drug, and yet was promoted as helping reduce aggression in the elderly by sedating them.

But besides calming your grandparent's irritability, it could create problems of slurred speech, constipation, oversleeping, and in some patients, seizures and liver damage.

An undignified solution to growing old, and being treated as a burden or a bad tempered nuisance, someone who could only be coped with using pharmaceutical intervention.

When Aggressive Behavior In The Elderly Is The Problem

"Regardless of etiology the physician is often in the position of having to intervene in a potentially dangerous situation. Stabilizing the person's behavior must be the first concern." [1(Ancill)]

Loxapac May Be Particularly Beneficial For Elderly Patients With Aggressive Behavior

- Loxapac controls aggressive behavior in both elderly patients and patients suffering from acute schizophrenia. [2-4]
- Loxapac produces significant improvement of psychopathology and social functioning in elderly patients compared to haloperidol. [2(Petrie)]

"When treating these [elderly] patients the physician should choose *as specific acting a drug as possible*, avoiding those with a wide range of actions and resulting side-effects." [1(Ancill)]

- Loxapac has fewer extrapyramidal side-effects than haloperidol. [5(Paprocki)]
- Loxapac also has less sedation, orthostatic hypotension and anticholinergic side-effects than lower potency neuroleptics, chlorpromazine and thioridazine. [6(Bernstein)]

Dosage Flexibility For Elderly Patients

- Lower initial doses and more gradual titration are recommended for elderly and debilitated patients. [7]

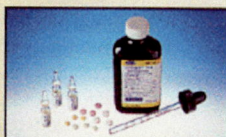

Suggested initial oral dose = 5 mg BID

LOXAPAC

loxapine succinate

Effective Control Of Aggression With Moderate Side-Effects

Lederle

Cyanamid Canada Inc. Markham

AN ORIGINAL BRAND NAME MEDICINE

PAAB CUPP

*Loxapac is a Registered Trademark of Cyanamid Canada Inc.

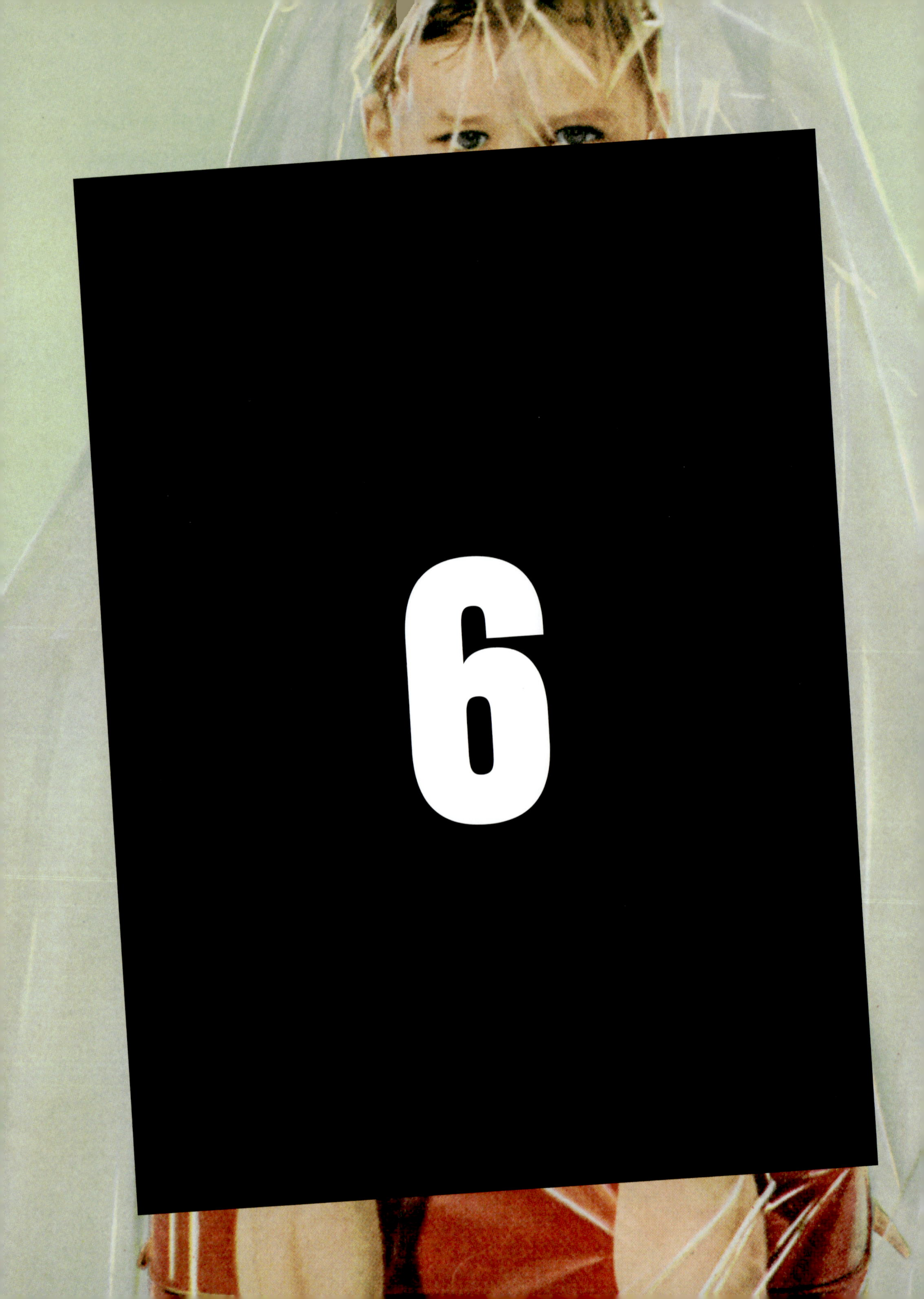
6

FAT BANISHED WITH SANITISED TAPE WORMS...

Jenny has been in orbit since breakfast time.

From school she rushed off to a Girl Scout meeting, a trampoline class, and then the pep rally.

Jenny needs a sugarless, energyless soft drink like a Beatle needs a hairpiece.

Two-four-six-eight, what does she appreciate?

Sugar.

It quenches fatigue.

NOTE TO MOTHERS

How much energy does your child get from the synthetic sweetener in a bottle of diet soft drink? Exactly none. And how much energy does she need? You tell us—and ask yourself if you're doing her a favor when you stock the refrigerator with no-sugar soft drinks. She'll drink them—her thirst craves anything that's cold and wet. But if you want her to have the energy she needs, you'll bring home the kind with sugar.

SUGAR'S GOT WHAT IT TAKES

...18 calories per teaspoon—and it's all energy

Sugar Information, Inc.

For sweetness with energy, get beet or cane sugar

1

Sugar Information Council, Leo Burnett Agency, *Life*, 1964

Sugar, asbestos, radioactivity and tapeworms are good for you...

During the late 1950s reduced calorie artificial sweeteners such as saccharine were becoming an attractive replacement for sugar, and increasingly being adopted for a variety of food products.

They were marketed as diet-friendly, and as their popularity spread sugar manufacturers felt threatened by this unexpected new competitor.

They formed the Sugar Information Council to launch an advertising campaign aimed at illustrating the benefits of sugar consumption.

Sugar was to now be seen as an energising product, that reduces fatigue, and also as a natural and effective dietary aid that curbs appetites.

They argued that if your blood sugar level is low, your appetite increases, and you may also feel tired.

Therefore, they claimed, sugar can help to make you feel full, as it enters the bloodstream faster than any other food and is quickly turned into energy.

Advertisements portrayed children cheerleading and trampolining, stating that 'sugar quenches fatigue'. It would be a clear sign of poor parenting to force substitute sugar products on your offspring.

But the antipathy to sugar became remorseless. In John Yudkin's influential 1972 book *Pure, White and Deadly*, the conclusion was clear – 'consumption of sugar is closely associated with long-term disease'.

In *Sweet Poison: Why Sugar Is Ruining Our Health* Victoria Lambert claimed that 'sugar, whether added to food by you or the manufacturer, is the greatest threat to human health, bar none'.

Advertising was also used to promote one of the worst advances of science: asbestos.[236]

'The magic mineral of the Middle Ages,' this fibrous material was a boon to building construction as it was cheap, rat-proof, and practically indestructible.

Are you making your children pay for your weight problem?

If you're trying to lose weight by stocking the house with sugarless soft drinks, remember one thing. Your children will drink them too. Their thirst craves anything that's cold and wet.

But their bodies need much more. Energy. And that they'll never get from an artificial sweetener.

Now let's get back to you, and that diet of yours. Unless you make a career out of drinking soft drinks, saving calories with synthetic pops is a little like trying to reduce by getting a haircut.

Besides, you need sugar, too. Particularly when you're dieting.

Sugar in a soft drink does two nice things for you: 1) it satisfies those between-meal hunger pangs, and 2) it gives you the va-va-voom you need for all those exercises.

Sugar quenches fatigue

...18 calories per teaspoon—and it's all energy

Note to Mothers:

Exhaustion may be dangerous—especially to children who haven't learned to avoid it by pacing themselves. Exhaustion opens the door a little wider to the bugs and ailments that are always lying in wait. Sugar puts back energy fast—offsets exhaustion. Synthetic sweeteners put back nothing. Energy is the first requirement of life. Play safe with your young ones—make sure they get sugar every day.

Sugar Information, Inc. P. O. Box 2664, Grand Central Station, New York, N. Y. 10017

For sweetness with energy, get beet or cane sugar

8

What was not known, as the product had not been adequately tested, was that exposure to asbestos could be lethal. Embedded in our homes, schools, offices and shops, it was eventually found to create cancers that can take a decade to develop.

Politicians acted swiftly to have it banned and removed everywhere, when it was discovered that even the Houses of Parliament were contaminated by asbestos.

A product that would be a little harder to swallow today, though not unheard of, was sanitised tapeworms.

Advertised for 'nutrient absorption' it did what it said on the packet: the worms fed off the digested food in your stomach.

The first early advertisements promised: 'No diet, no baths, no exercise. Fat – the enemy that is shortening your life – banished. How? With sanitized tapeworms – jar-packed'.[240]

They continued to be marketed in this way into the 1930s.

Let this magic mineral, **ASBESTOS**, protect the buildings on your farm!

JOHNS·MANVILLE
JM
PRODUCTS

Asbestos! The magic mineral of the Middle Ages. Today, still a "magic" mineral; fireproof, rot-proof, and practically indestructible. When combined with portland cement it is manufactured into products which are especially important on the farm, because they provide permanent protection against fire, weather, and wear. Read this folder. Learn how to put this magic mineral to work on your farm.

Radioactivity.
It's been in the family for generations.

In fact, scientists can tell us just how old our remote ancestors are by measuring the radioactivity still in the bones of prehistoric cave dwellers.

Radioactivity dating is possible because virtually everything on earth—food, air, water, man himself—is radioactive and always has been.

Obviously, radiation is nothing new. Using nuclear power plants to generate electricity isn't exactly new either.

We've been doing it for 15 years.

And experience has shown that a person living next door to a nuclear power plant for a year would be exposed to less additional radiation than by making one round-trip coast-to-coast flight.

Understanding that nuclear power plants are safe, clean places to make electricity is important, because the demand for electric energy continues to grow. And nuclear power is one of the best ways we have for meeting it.

Our country's ability to do the work that needs to be done will depend on an adequate supply of electricity. There's no time to waste. New generating facilities must be built, and built in a way compatible with our environment.

We'll continue working to do this. But we need your understanding today to meet tomorrow's needs.

The people at your Investor-Owned Electric Light and Power Companies:

For names of sponsoring companies, write to Power Companies, 1045 Avenue of the Americas, New York, New York 10019

According to the NHS 'tapeworms tend to be flat, segmented and ribbon-like and can be caught by eating raw contaminated pork, beef or fish. The worm can grow to many feet in length inside your body.

One dangerous complication that can occur is called neuro-cysticercosis, an infection brought on by tapeworm larvae. It affects the brain and central nervous system, causing headaches and effecting sight. It can also cause meningitis, epilepsy or dementia.'

Bewilderingly, the 1950s heralded an era in American consumer culture when radioactivity was exciting.

Although today we use radiation for x-rays and for cancer treatments, at that time it was a new and innovative treatment that had hundreds of applications.

Late in 1944 when it became clear that Germany would not win the war, the German Auer Company diverted thorium supplies from the Nazi atomic program towards the use of nuclear materials in cosmetics.

They developed Doramad radioactive toothpaste to make your teeth 'glisten white and hinder bacteria'.

This spurred other companies to follow their lead, and a line of beauty products were created under the name Thoradia.

They included facial creams, soaps and face powder.

The Radium Emanator was one of many devices created to enable people to make their own radioactive water, with a myriad of benefits.

Up until the 1960s shoe stores would measure a child's foot by placing it into an x-ray fluoroscope.

The bones in the feet were made visible to both the shoe salesman and the customer, while at the same time being contaminated by leaking radiation.

What also started leaking was news about its deadly side-effects.

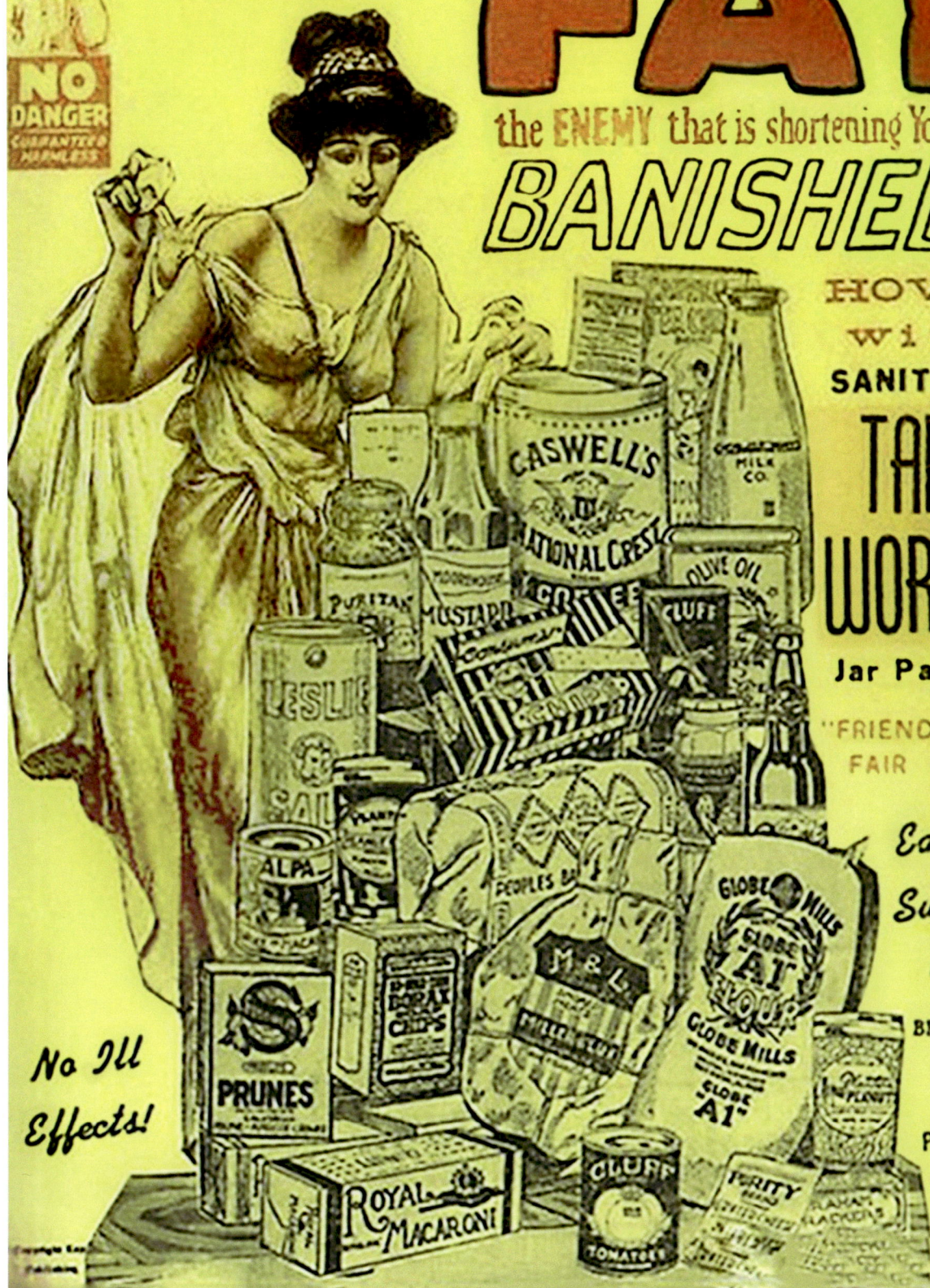

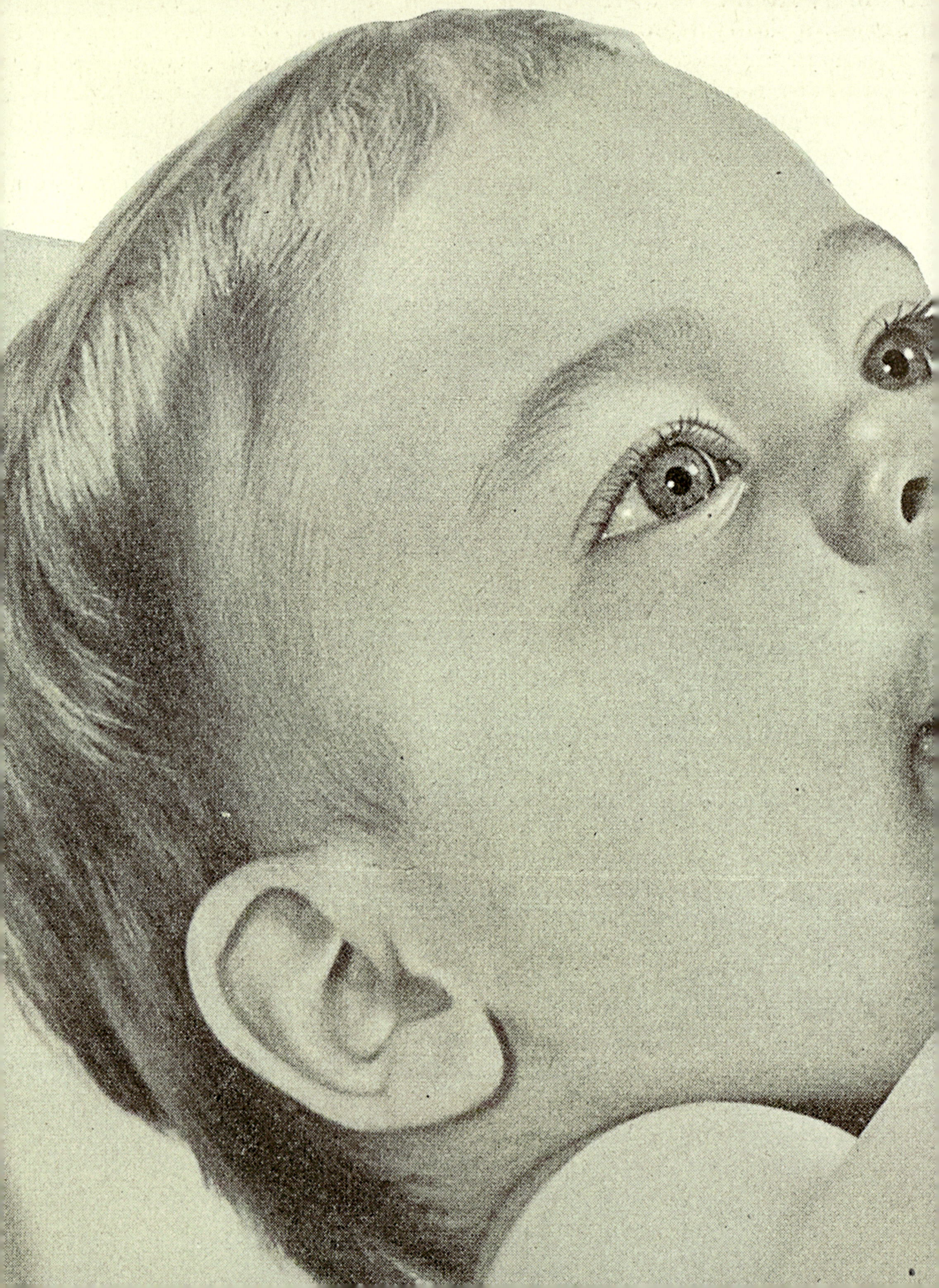

Iver Johnson's Arms & Cycle Works, *Harpers*, 1904

Guns, cocaine, beer, 7-Up and sun lamps are good for infants...

It was in the years between the two World Wars that children were first groomed to become consumers.

At a moment of historical change, with an economy being driven by child labour, it was decided to give children the right to have a childhood.

More often than not, children from impoverished backgrounds were primarily valued by the amount of income they could generate for their families.

The US government actively helped in defining childhood when in 1929 Herbert Hoover sponsored a White House study on Child Health and Protection.

The conference report, *The Home and the Child*, concluded that children were individuals with needs that were separate from their parents.

Parents were advised to provide each child with their own belongings such as furniture, toys, and playrooms.

It was noted that 'generally a sleeping room is desirable' and it was decreed that children should be taken shopping for 'things' and allowed to 'pick them out for themselves'.

Advertising was of course still aimed at parents, with helpful suggestions for fulfilling their child's needs.

This preceded the era of 'pester power' when marketing was targeted directly at children, hoping to encourage them to nag parents to buy them your product.

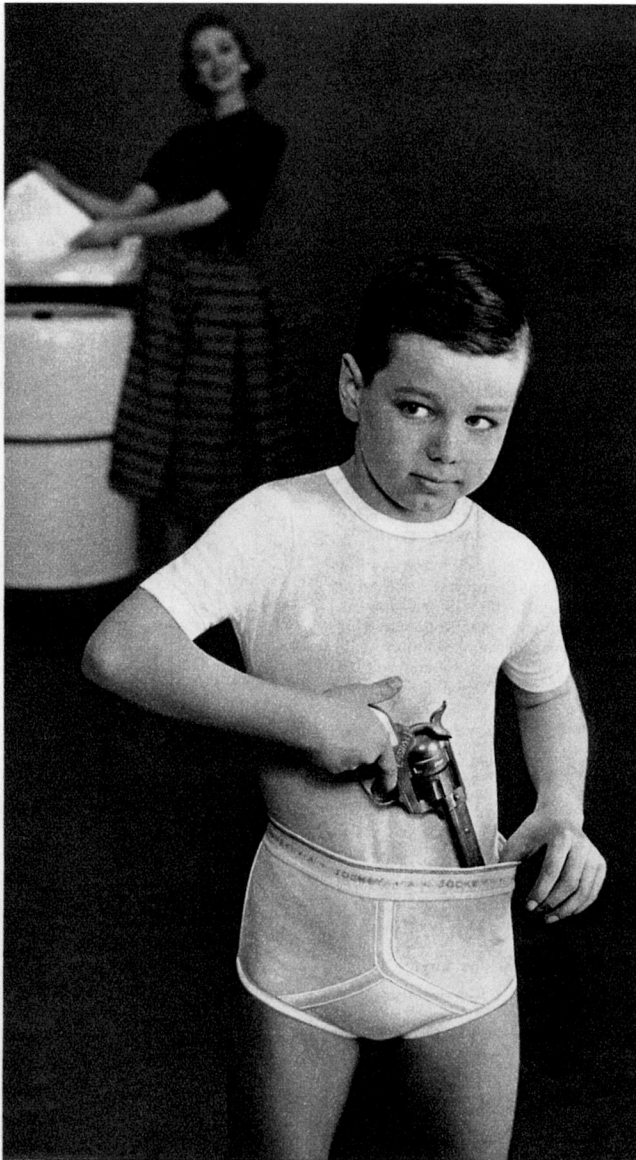

They keep their fit!

Jockey junior briefs *keep* their fit—wash after wash! Special elastic waistband never droops, never sags, for it's guaranteed for the life of the garment! Nobelt strip rubber (around outer thighs only) means no-gap leg openings that *never bind.* Shaped seat and double thick seamless crotch help give the comfort that comes only with Jockey—first underwear tailored to fit the male figure! Matching Jockey T-shirt has nylon-content neck—*holds* its shape!

Jockey
BRAND
junior brief and T-shirt

made only by *Coopers*

known the world over by this symbol ⚶ Cooper's, Incorporated–Kenosha. Wis. Licensees and registered users: Canada: J.R. Moodie Company, Limited: Australia: Speedo Knitting Mills: British Isles: Lyle & Scott: New Zealand: Lane. Walker. Rudkin: Switzerland: Vollmoeller: France: Verdier: Colombia: Textiles, Ego: Italy: Sacit: Denmark: Taco: So. Africa: Ninian & Lester: Germany: Volma: Austria: Josef Huber's Erben: Ireland: Dublin Shirt & Collar Company: Mexico: Manufacturera Rinbros.

Jockey Cooper, Henri, Hurst & McDonald, Inc. Agency, 1956

COCAINE
TOOTHACHE DROPS

Instantaneous Cure!

PRICE 15 CENTS.

Prepared by the

LLOYD MANUFACTURING CO.

219 HUDSON AVE., ALBANY, N. Y.

For sale by all Druggists.

Iver Johnson was a US firearms manufacturer who also produced bicycles and motorcycles from 1871 to 1993.[243]

Their marketing campaigns sought a new and younger generation of gun owners, proposing that using a gun literally is child's play.

The irony of their advertisement's two claims can be seen when read side by side: 'they shoot straight and kill' – 'absolutely safe'.

Cocaine Toothache Drops were thought to be an 'instantaneous cure!'[247] and cocaine was being marketed as a 'new anaesthetic now used so extensively throughout Europe and this country by Physicians, Surgeons and Dentists'.

It had been discovered far earlier that the indigenous people of Bolivia, Peru and Colombia would chew the leaves of the coca plant for its medicinal and energising properties; the substance was brought over to Europe in large quantities, much like tea.

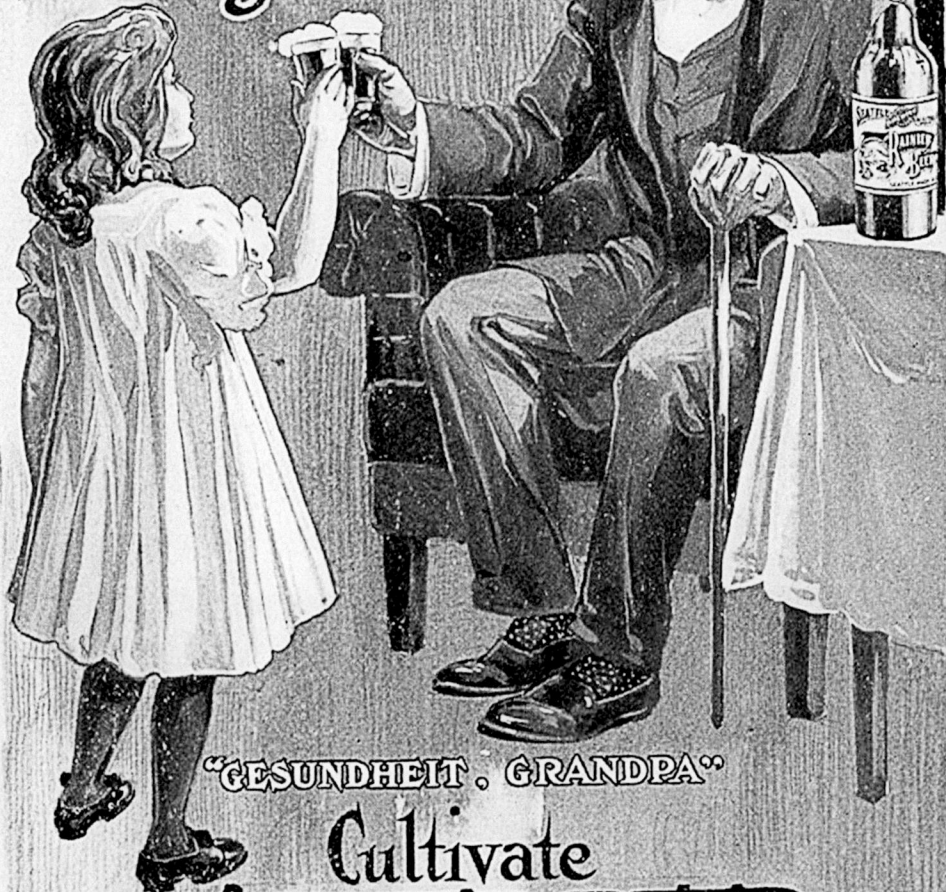

In Germany, Dr Albert Niemann isolated its active ingredients to transform it into the stimulant popular today. He named the substance 'cocaine'.

The drug's anaesthetic properties were discovered in the late 1900s and became used in eye, nose, and throat surgery. It was only later that physicians became aware of cocaine's psychoactive properties.

Cocaine later had a renaissance in the drug culture of the 1970s, becoming an iconic symbol of success and driving ambition.

But soon the drug was available at a greatly reduced price, expanding the market to epidemic proportions globally.

The golden tan many people aspire to didn't start off as a fashion statement or as a sign of wealth.

"Is there a baby in the house?"

Switch on a G-E Sunlamp and let the whole family bask in ultra-violet radiation . . . the chief natural source of vitamin D.

BRING ultra-violet radiation indoors this winter where you can really enjoy its benefits in solid comfort!

The new General Electric Sunlamp makes it so easy. You can rest or read—work or play—in perfect freedom. No goggles are needed if you don't look directly into the light.

Your doctor will tell you that everyone needs vitamin D. Especially babies and growing children. They *have* to have it to build strong bones and teeth. But hardly any foods have any vitamin D at all and winter sunlight is woefully weak in ultra-violet rays.

The effect of the ultra-violet rays of the G-E Sunlamp is so similar to that of the summer sun that doctors recommend it as one way to overcome this scarcity of vitamin D. Note that it bears the Seal of Acceptance of the Council on Physical Therapy of the American Medical Association.

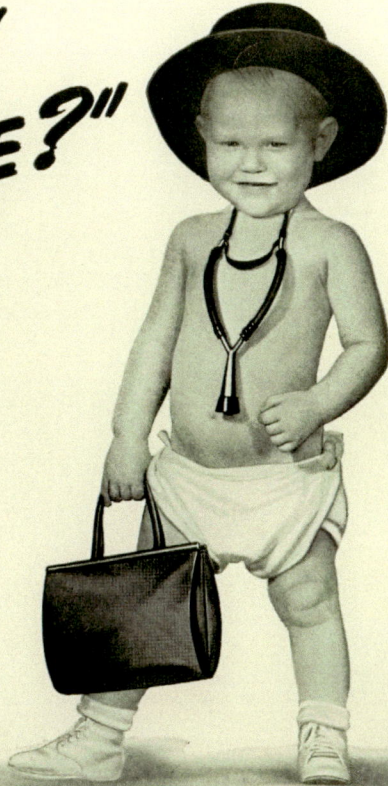

EVERY DAY IS "SUN" DAY ALL WINTER LONG!

"Winter Vacation" tan is easy to have through short daily exposure under a General Electric Sunlamp while you shave, dress, rest or read. No wonder it's the largest selling sunlamp of its kind in America.

Natural bloom cannot be equalled by make-up. A few minutes each day under a General Electric Sunlamp—and your complexion takes on a lovely freshness. Ultra-violet rays also help your teeth to keep sound.

He's lucky his folks know the value of vitamin D. You can make sure *your* baby is getting plenty of vitamin D by turning on the General Electric Sunlamp for a few minutes every day while he plays or sleeps.

See the General Electric Sunlamp today at leading department stores and other G-E dealers. Priced from $29.95 (slightly higher in western region). Most stores offer a budget plan.

GENERAL ⊕ ELECTRIC
Sunlamps

If there's a baby in the house

Send for the very latest novelty for keeping a dramatic record of your child's growth—the General Electric Sunlamp Tel-A-Hite Tape, printed in full colors. Simple, easy, permanent. Use coupon below.

General Electric Co.,
Advertising Dept., EG-181, Bridgeport, Conn.
Please send me the General Electric Sunlamp Tel-A-Hite Tape and "JUST WHAT THE DOCTOR ORDERED," your newest booklet on the necessity of vitamin D. I am enclosing 10¢ to cover postage and handling.

Name..

Address..

City...State...........

NO GOGGLES REQUIRED
...avoid looking directly into the light

AMERICAN MEDICAL ASSN. ACCEPTED COUNCIL ON PHYSICAL THERAPY

35

General Electric, Batten, Barton, Durstine & Osborn Agency, *Life*, 1941

Watch "Soldiers of Fortune"!
For exciting adventure, see this
7-Up TV show every week.

Copyright 1955 by The Seven-Up Company

Why we have the youngest customers in the business

This young man is 11 months old—and he isn't our youngest customer by any means.

For 7-Up is so pure, so wholesome, you can even give it to babies and feel good about it. Look at the back of a 7-Up bottle. Notice that all our ingredients are listed. (That isn't required of soft drinks, you know —but we're proud to do it and we think you're pleased that we do.)

By the way, Mom, when it comes to toddlers—if they like to be coaxed to drink their milk, try this: Add 7-Up to the milk in equal parts, pouring the 7-Up gently into the milk. It's a wholesome combination—and it works! Make 7-Up your family drink. *You like it . . . it likes you!*

Avoid imitations served from taps or cup-machines. Seven-Up is sold in bottles only.

Nothing *does it* like Seven-Up!

7-Up, J. Walter Thomspon Agency, *Saturday Evening Post*, 1955

In 1960 the DuPont Health Tan Sun Lamp was promoted as being beneficial to babies at two weeks old.[252]

Sun lamps were readily available and became popular with many, and were also used widely for medical purposes. People trusted the product and never questioned the after-effects of their artificial suns, in an era before links to skin cancer were acknowledged.

In fact there appeared to be much evidence of the health advantages.

It had been demonstrated by scientists that 'vitamin D is necessary to build up the bones with calcium and this process is triggered by ultraviolet light'.

The research study was received with great excitement and children began to receive sun lamp therapy all over Britain, Europe and the US.

Mom says
I'm so fresh
and so clean
(*sometimes*)—
she ought to
wrap me in
Cellophane
to keep me
that way.

Everything's at its best in Cellophane

- Cellophane keeps things clean
- Cellophane keeps things fresh
- Cellophane lets you see what you buy

DU PONT
Cellophane

DU PONT

BETTER THINGS FOR BETTER LIVING
...THROUGH CHEMISTRY

Watch "Du Pont Cavalcade Theater" on Television

DuPont, Batten, Barton, Durstine & Osborn Agency , 1956

Today, the devastating consequences of ultraviolet light have been made clear – using a sunbed regularly under the age of 30 increases cancer risks by 75%.

The rates of malignant melanoma in the UK have more than quadrupled in the last three decades, with many adults who were subjected to sun lamp treatment as children becoming victims.

When the baby swigging 7-Up advertisement appeared, the soda drink that had originally been called "Bib-Label Lithiated Lemon-Lime Soda" had been rebranded with its new catchier name.[253]

One of its ingredients was lithium, the powerful mood-enhancing drug prescribed for severe clinical depression.

The campaign treated 7-Up as an elixir for crying babies, and mothers were encouraged to treat their baby in the same way a doctor would treat a patient with depression or bipolar disorder.

The advertisement reads: 'This young man is 11 months old – and he isn't our youngest customer by any means. For 7-Up is so pure, so wholesome, you can even give it to babies and feel good about it'.

Unsurprisingly, the US Food and Drug Administration decided to ban the use of lithium in beer and soft drinks, though they took their time in getting round to doing so.

It's the <u>happiest</u> flying...from the ground up!

...ANOTHER REASON WHY
MORE AIRLINES CHOOSE
THE DC·8
THAN ANY OTHER
JETLINER

For more than forty years, the Douglas Aircraft Company has been in the business of making flying a pleasure for you with a series of famous airplanes.

Today, in the jet age, Douglas brings you the DC-8—an advanced jet aircraft, designed from the first with *people* in mind. If you've had your first flight in a DC-8 you know what a happy experience flying can be.

Pilots, too, speak of the DC-8 as a truly great airplane. Its stability in flight, its easy behavior on landings and take-offs, make the DC-8 a joy to handle—and a dream to fly in.

So make a date with the DC-8. You'll fly the miles away in a happy frame of mind in this favorite jetliner.

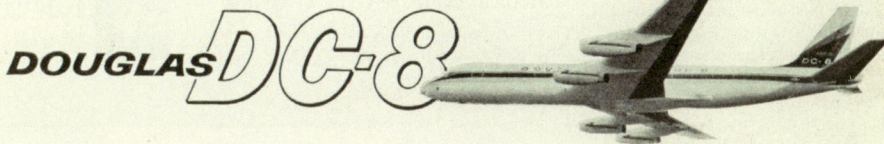

DOUGLAS DC·8

Douglas DC-8, J. Walter Thompson Agency, *Saturday Evening Post*, 1960

Edwin Grove discovered a way
to bottle quinine and make it
nearly tasteless, although there
was a hint of the sweet syrup
and lemon used to mask the
flavour.

It was not sold as a cure, but as a
preventative for malaria, chills
and fever.

Initially given to troops fighting
in mosquito-infested lands, it
became wildly popular with the
public and at its height sold more
bottles than Coca-Cola.

In those days, a demonstration of
health and wealth was obesity.

Only the rich didn't have to do
manual work, so being heavyset
equated with success.

Grove's Tonic was perceived as
an excellent way to fatten
yourself up, and achieve a
prosperous well-fed appearance.

MAKES CHILDREN AND ADULTS AS FAT AS PIGS.
NO CURE NO PAY
Price 50 Cents.
GROVE'S
TASTELESS CHILL TONIC
ON THE MARKET OVER 20 YEARS
1½ MILLION BOTTLES SOLD LAST YEAR

"**Mary was so fidgety she couldn't concentrate . . .**

. . . I was shocked to find that harsh toilet tissue was the cause"

"I WAS worried when Mary's teacher told me she was restless in school and couldn't seem to concentrate.

"When I asked Mary what was the matter she complained of an itching. I asked a friend's advice at Mother's Club that afternoon. She said it was probably caused by harsh or impure toilet tissue, and recommended ScotTissue.

"So I bought some ScotTissue. It looked very pure and soft. In a few days Mary's trouble had entirely disappeared. I was amazed to find that toilet tissue could cause so much discomfort."

EXPERIENCES LIKE THIS are common. Harsh tissue can cause serious inflammation. Women and girls especially, because of their peculiar requirements, need a soft, highly absorbent tissue—such as ScotTissue or Waldorf.

Made to the same standards of purity as absorbent cotton, these famous health tissues cleanse and dry thoroughly, safely. Highly absorbent, they assure at all times an immaculate condition. They are extremely soft—soothing to even the most sensitive skin.

ScotTissue or Waldorf in your bathroom protects the health of every member of your family. Always keep a supply on hand. Scott Paper Company, Chester, Pennsylvania.

SCOTTISSUE— the soft, pure white, 1000-sheet roll

WALDORF—the soft, popular-priced, cream-colored roll

Scott Tissues *Soft as Old Linen*

Scott Tissues, J. Walter Thompson Agency, 1933

Why was mommy cross?

Scott Paper Company is credited with introducing toilet paper in a perforated roll. The Scott brothers did not want to brand the product with the family name, feeling nervous about the unpleasant association with an embarrassing topic; it was a more conservative time.

Selecting the brand name Waldorf, they gradually introduced the Scott name when they felt the new notion of toilet rolls had lost any disagreeable undertones.

They also relied on high profile advertising to support distribution of their product, with stores initially refusing to display it and customers hesitant about asking for it.

Fortunately, the company's timing coincided with the increased use of indoor plumbing, and by promoting the product as a health aid they made it more generally acceptable.

People soon discovered how convenient Scott toilet rolls were to use, rather than bundles of individual coarse paper squares, or old newspapers.

Perception grew that this new way of toilet cleansing had helped halt the spread of cholera, dysentery, typhoid and other diseases, particularly when outbreaks of these infections began to dramatically reduce.

It was important that their tissues could be flushed down the toilet bowl to disintegrate, impossible if using normal paper, which had to disposed of by other means.

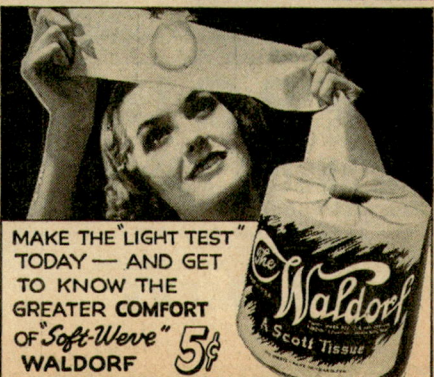

By 1925 they were the leading toilet roll provider in the world, and had started promoting their brand more openly, using the slogan 'soft as old linen'.

Even during the Depression, Scott Paper factories operated at full capacity, with the need for toilet paper becoming a fixture in the public eye.

By 1955, it became the first toilet tissue to advertise on television, promoting the comfort of its two-ply softer paper.

Over the centuries, mankind has moved from dried bamboo pulp, to rags, to large leaves, to mass pro-duction of early coarse paper, to cutting-up copies of the giant Sears catalogue, to the supersoft, lightly scented colourful toilet rolls of today.

Scott took advantage of the discomfort customers endured with scratchy paper that could irritate or inflame their bottoms; they focused directly on this problem with heavyweight advertising support.

It remained a brand leader for generations, fighting off stiff competition from other brands.

Deservedly so, for having fought so hard to introduce the world to a product we now all take for granted: the humble toilet roll.

Is your washroom breeding

Bolshe

Introducing the Flip 'N Style™ hair dryer. Even if you can't use it it's fun to have.

Of course, it dries your hair. If you happen to think that hair is fashionable. But it's also a nice replacement for your teddy bear. It comes in three terrific colors to go with any bedspread. And it doesn't just sit around like your old teddy.

Because the Flip 'N Style™ flips for you. Open. And closed. So when you're through drying (your fingernails, if your hair hasn't grown in), slip it into its attractive case. Then slip it into your attractive purse. So if you run into a cloudburst or fall into a swimming pool, you're prepared.

The Flip 'N Style™ has what you need to style your hair. 350 watts of hot-air power. And a switch to turn on cool air when your hair is dry, but not completely styled.

So give your hair a chance. Let it have as much fun as the rest of you. With a Panasonic Flip 'N Style.™

Panasonic.
just slightly ahead of our time.

200 Park Ave., N.Y. 10017. For your nearest Panasonic dealer, call toll free 800 243-6000. In Conn., 1-800 882-6500.

Panasonic, Ted Bates Agency, *Teen Magazine*, 1972

Let's get down to business...

During the 1950s and 60s, an era of consumption anxiety overwhelmed consumers.

New and improved products were continually being offered by manufacturers, and selling techniques became increasingly sophisticated, employing generational and demographic marketing.

Goods unavailable or in short supply during World War II were again in abundance; clothing, refrigerators, televisions and automobiles enjoyed an ever increasing demand.

People started discovering an enticing choice of many fancier products.

The Panasonic Flip'N Style Blow Dryer was so small it could easily sit in the palm of your hand. Mainly targeted at teens, the product's ability to fit into a handbag was its key selling point.

It was also intended to be pleasurable rather than being merely practical.

Featuring a bald model, it claimed 'Even if you can't use it, it is fun to have!'

Of course, such an image would be unthinkable in later years, when cancer therapies created hair loss.

In reality, chemotherapy and radiology treatments were already being utilised in American hospitals in the 1960s, and this advertisement should have been unthinkable even then.

Equally inconceivable would be a campaign for a beer dispenser accessory for your car – 'Your favourite beverage on tap, all of the time.'[277]

And in those more prurient times Munsingwear advertising featured two gentlemen in their underpants grasping each other.

"Let's Get Down to Business"

● "STRETCHY-SEAT" is a Munsingwear exclusive. It is a special horizontal panel knitted to give *up and down*. No other underwear has "STRETCHY-SEAT." Men find it so comfortable they keep coming back for more. That's good business.

"Stretchy-Seat" *is an exclusive feature of Munsingwear's* SKIT. *Trunks, Shorts, Longies and Shin-highs.*

MUNSINGWEAR'S
MUNSINGWEAR INCORPORATED
"STRETCHY-SEAT"
REG. TRADE-MARK.
UNDERWEAR FOR MEN

Advertised in **LIFE**

MUNSINGWEAR, INC., MINNEAPOLIS • NEW YORK • CHICAGO • LOS ANGELES

4

MEN'S WEAR

Munsingwear, Kenyon & Eckhardt, Inc. Agency, 1939

EACH DAY HUMBLE SUPPLIES ENOUGH ENERG

This giant glacier has remained unmelted for centuries. Yet, the petroleum energy Humble supplies—
converted into heat—could melt it at the rate of 80 tons each second! To meet the nation's growing n
for energy, Humble has applied science to nature's resources to become America's Leading Energy Comp
Working wonders with oil through research, Humble provides energy in many forms—to help heat our ho
power our transportation, and to furnish industry with a great variety of versatile chemicals. Stop at a Hum
station for famous Esso Extra gasoline, and see why the "Happy Motoring"® Sign is the World's First Cho

TAKU GLACIER, ALASKA, IS A RIVER OF ICE STRETCHING 270 SQUARE MILES. YET THE PETROLEUM ENERGY HUMBLE SUPPLIES AMERICA COULD MELT IT AT THE RATE OF 7 MILLION TONS A DAY!

O MELT 7 MILLION TONS OF GLACIER!

HUMBLE
OIL & REFINING COMPANY
America's Leading **Ɛnergy** Company

Esso

R2

Humble, *Life*, 1962

Any homoerotic reading of the
image would have remained
unnoticed or unspoken.

Advertising portrayed society's
economic growth, its technological
advances and its renewed optimism.

Becoming a two-car family
was promoted vigorously, and
automobiles became the most
heavily advertised products,
exceeding tobacco, toiletries
and foodstuffs.

Drivers were encouraged to
view their vehicles as extensions
of themselves.

Stylish designs and exciting new
improvements arrived each year –
air conditioning, electric windows
and seats, power steering, built in
audio systems – making it seem
vital to renew your car frequently,
unrelated to any performance
considerations.

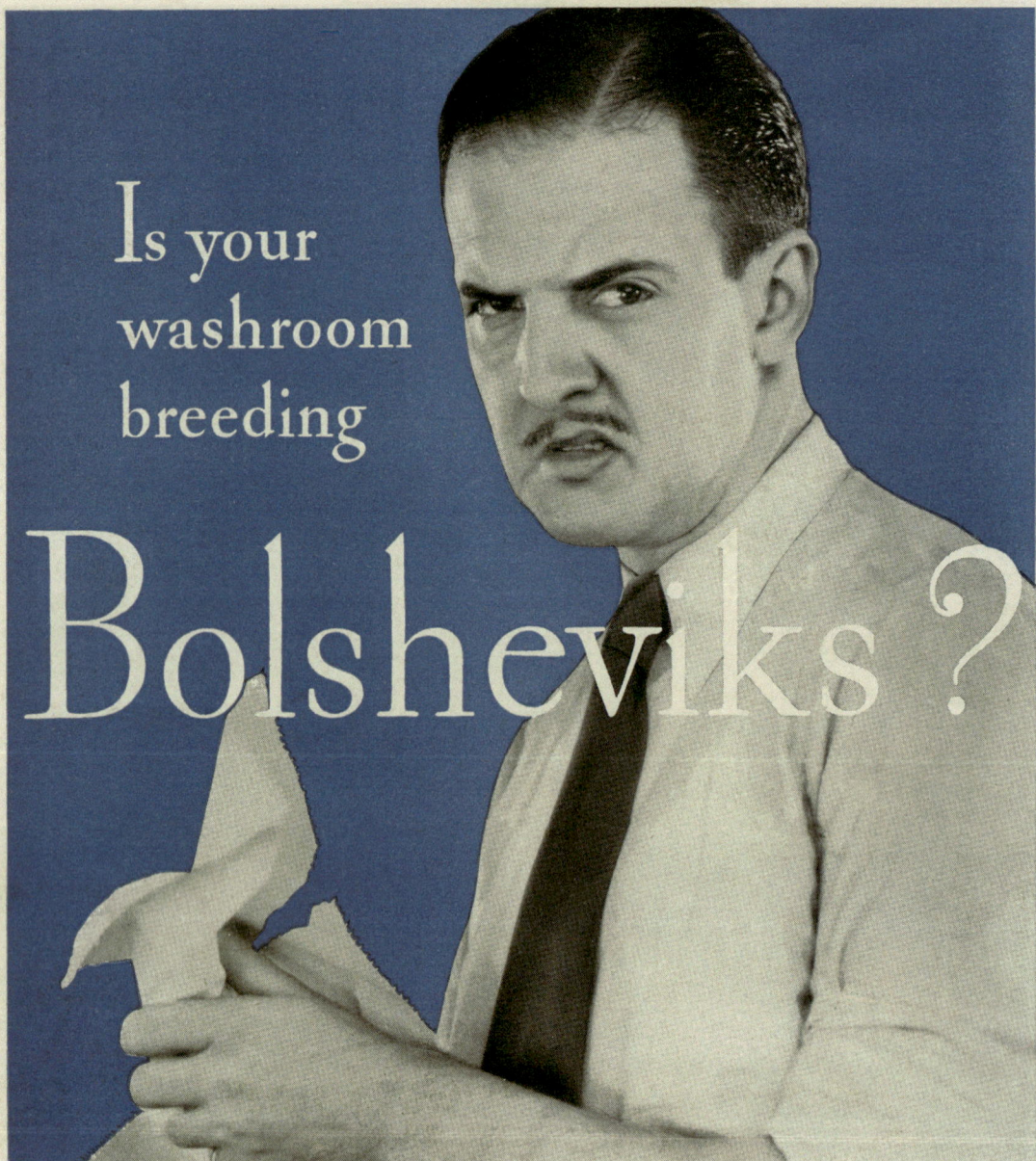

Is your washroom breeding

Bolsheviks ?

Employees lose respect for a company that fails to provide decent facilities for their comfort

TRY wiping your hands six days a week on harsh, cheap paper towels or awkward, unsanitary roller towels — and maybe you, too, would grumble.

Towel service is just one of those small, but important courtesies — such as proper air and lighting — that help build up the goodwill of your employees.

That's why you'll find clothlike Scot-Tissue Towels in the washrooms of large, well-run organizations such as R.C.A. Victor Co., Inc., National Lead Co. and Campbell Soup Co.

ScotTissue Towels are made of "thirsty fibre". . . an amazing cellulose product that drinks up moisture 12 times as fast as ordinary paper towels. They feel soft and pliant as a linen towel. Yet they're so strong and tough in texture they won't crumble or go to pieces . . . even when they're wet.

And they cost less, too — because one is enough to dry the hands — instead of three or four.

Write for free trial carton. Scott Paper Company, Chester, Pennsylvania.

ScotTissue Towels - *really* dry !

Scott Tissues, J. Walter Thompson Agency, Time, 1931

The rise in the number of new homes stimulated the need for an array of appliances and furnishings to constantly fill them.

Humble Oil proudly announced that they were melting seven million tons of glacier every day, in the effort to provide consumers affordable home heating and cooling, and cheap fuel for automobiles.[273]

This was clearly an era when environmental concerns actually concerned very few.

Industrial capitals like Pittsburgh, fondly known as 'Smoky City' had an elongated history of polluted atmosphere.

The issue was never taken very seriously by the inhabitants of Pittsburgh, as they did not consider their murky air a threat.

Besides providing mass employment, industrial chimneys constantly filling the skies were regarded as a prosperous symbol of productivity, and many even believed that smoke encouraged crops to grow.

Pittsburgh emerged from its hazy darkness by the end of the 1980s, as many iron and steel factories collapsed, at last revealing the city's attractive skyline.

7

WOMEN
ARE
TEACHABLE:
A
HANDBOOK
FOR
EMPLOYERS,
1943,
RCA
CORPORATION...

WOMEN ARE TEACHABLE

WHEN YOU SUPERVISE A WOMAN

Make clear her part in the process or product on which she works.

●

Allow for her lack of familiarity with machine processes.

●

See that her working set-up is comfortable, safe and convenient.

●

Start her right by kindly and careful supervision.

●

Avoid horseplay or "kidding"; she may resent it.

●

Suggest rather than reprimand.

●

When she does a good job, tell her so.

●

Listen to and aid her in her work problems.

Women are teachable...

World War II brought females into factories, often for the first time.

Brochures were routinely produced to inform managers about the best way to supervise their new female staff.

Articles such as 'Tips to Hiring Women', published in the 1943 edition of *Transportation* magazine, were fairly commonplace. It offers sympathetic advice for male bosses:

1. Give every girl an adequate number of rest periods during the day. You have to unfortunately make allowances for feminine psychology. A girl has more confidence and is more efficient if she can keep her hair tidied, apply fresh lipstick and do her nails.

WOMEN ARE CAREFUL

WHENEVER YOU EMPLOY A WOMAN

Limit her hours to 8 a day, and 48 a week, if possible.

●

Arrange brief rest periods in the middle of each shift.

●

Try to make nourishing foods available for lunch periods.

●

Try to provide a clean place to eat lunch, away from her workplace. Make pure and cool drinking water accessible.

●

See that toilet and rest-rooms are clean and adequate.

●

Watch work hazards—moving machinery; dust and fumes; improper lifting; careless housekeeping.

●

Provide properly adjusted work seats; good ventilation and lighting.

●

Recommend proper clothing for each job; safe, comfortable shoes; try to provide lockers and a place to change to work clothes.

●

Relieve a monotonous job with rest periods. If possible, use music during fatigue periods.

2. Older women who have never spent time outside their home may be cantankerous and fussy. Impress upon them the importance of friendliness and courtesy!

3. Pick young married women. They have more of a sense – usually – of responsibility, than the unmarried type. They are less likely to flirt.

4. General experience indicates that 'husky' girls – those on the heavy side – are more even-tempered and efficient that their underweight sisters.

5. Give each woman a special physical examination – one to cover female conditions. This step not only protects the property against lawsuits but reveals whether the potential female employee has any weaknesses that would make her mentally or physically unfit.

6. When possible – let the employee change from one job to another at some time during the working day. Women are less inclined to be nervous and like change!

7. Be tactful when issuing criticisms. Women are often sensitive; they can't just shrug off harsh words the way men do. Never ridicule a woman – it breaks her spirit.

8. Be considerate about using strong language around women. She'll grow to dislike her place of work if she hears too much swearing.

9. Get enough sizes in uniforms so that every girl will have a proper fit. This point can't be stressed too much in keeping women happy.

10. Women lack initiative in finding work for themselves – keep them busy with a daylong schedule.

When the United States entered World War II the most famous image of female patriotism in World War II emerged, Rosie the Riveter.

Rosie was a cultural icon representing the American women who worked in factories during the war, many of whom produced munitions and war supplies.

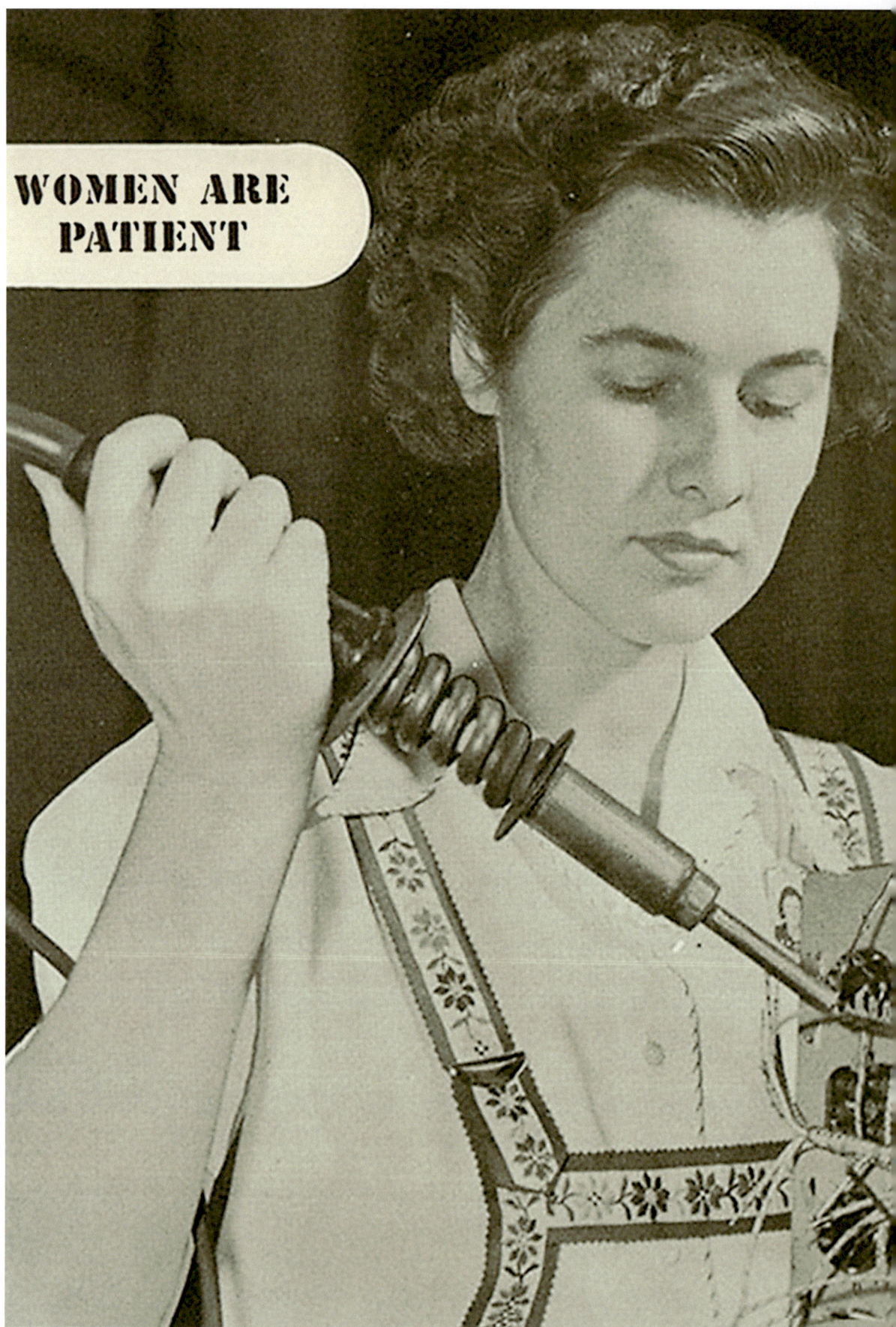

WHEN YOU PUT
A WOMAN TO WORK

Have a job breakdown for her job.

●

Consider her education, work experience and temperament in assigning her to that job.

●

Have the necessary equipment, tools and supplies ready for her.

●

Try out her capacity for and familiarity with the work.

●

Assign her to a shift in accordance with health, home obligations and transportation arrangements.

●

Place her in a group of workers with similar backgrounds and interests.

●

Inform her fully on health and safety rules, company policies, company objectives.

●

Be sure she knows the location of rest-rooms, lunch facilities, dispensaries.

●

Don't change her shift too often and never without notice.

Employed in male-dominated jobs, often with a labour component, a female workforce could don denim trousers, hardhats, and boots for the first time.

These working women changed the norms of fashion forever. Most found a way to incorporate their personal, often feminine identity into their work-wear, and chose the latest hair styles, accessories, and often heels.

Others preferred to adopt the styles of their male counterparts, sometimes even wearing their husband's clothing. Importantly, they shifted the trajectory of women into the workforce for the first time.

Simplicity and convenience was the key, as many women took to working in factories and on farms. 'Bright red lips help perk up a tired girl' it was claimed, and in the US lipsticks were considered as essential in the war effort – to keep morale up.

Recommendations included:

- Foundation – a shade darker than your natural.

- Powder – plenty of powder still, a lighter shade and patted on.

- Eyes – light medium brown around the eyes, with beige highlighting. Understated.

- Eyebrows – much thicker than in the 1930s. Vaseline can be used to groom to shape.

- Lashes – cake mascaras like Maybelline – applied with a brush.

- Rouge – rose colours applied out from the apples of your cheeks.

- Nails – Filed to a round point with the tips left unpainted.

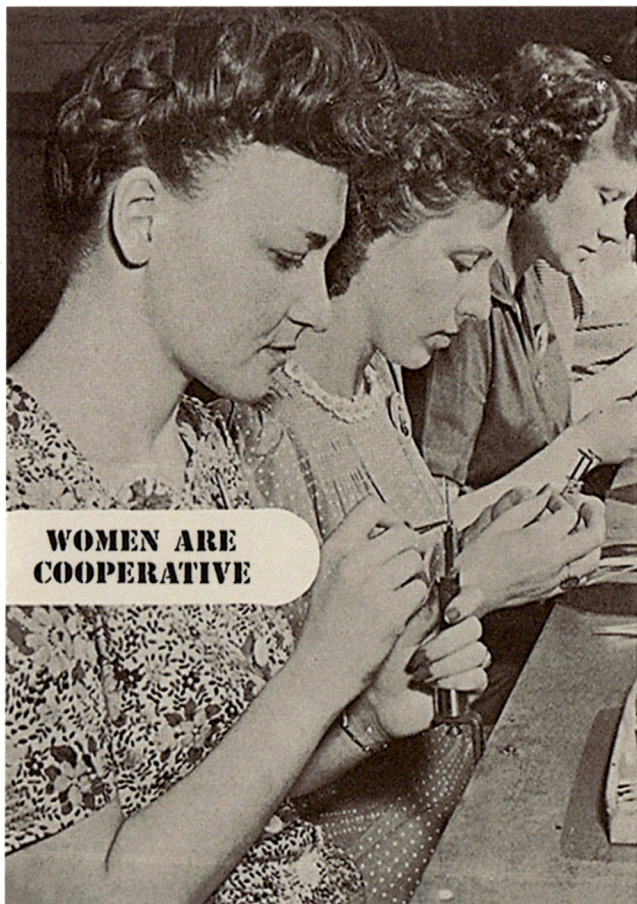

WOMEN ARE COOPERATIVE

FINALLY—CALL ON A TRAINED WOMAN COUNSELOR IN YOUR PERSONNEL DEPARTMENT

To find out what women workers think and want.

•

To discover personal causes of poor work, absenteeism, turnover.

•

To assist women workers in solving personal difficulties.

•

To interpret women's attitudes and actions.

•

To assist in adjusting women to their jobs.

In effect, World War II opened up new opportunities for women as vast numbers of men joined the armed services and went abroad; many positions could be filled that had been previously closed to them.

It had long been assumed women couldn't be considered for engineering and manufacturing jobs; now women built airplanes and warships, armaments and tanks, and worked in technical and scientific fields for the first time.

Most wanted to continue working after the war ended. But, of course, hundreds of thousands of men came back from serving in the military needing work, and there was widespread fear that there would be another depression once the wartime economy shut down.

Women were asked to do their part by leaving the job market. Many were fired from their jobs so the returning veterans could be re-employed.

Women were still decades away from any thoughts of equality in the workplace.

CREDITS

ean- It's
well

First published in 2015

Booth-Clibborn Editions

Editorial Director: Katherine Hawker

Editorial Associates: Natasha Hoare, Holly
Parkhouse, Prachi Gothi

Picture Research: Elena Goodinson

Design by Sean Murphy

Text copyright © Charles Saatchi, 2015

Book copyright © Booth-Clibborn Editions, 2015

Author photograph by James King

A Cataloguing-in-Publication record for this book
is available from the Publisher.

Booth-Clibborn Editions

Studio 83, 235 Earl's Court Road

London SW5 9FE

info@booth-clibborn.com

www.booth-clibborn.com

Printed and bound in China

ISBN 978-1-86154-372-1

Charles Saatchi founded the global advertising agency Saatchi & Saatchi in 1970 which grew to become the largest agency in the world. At the same time Saatchi began collecting art and later opened his first gallery a 30,000 square foot ex-paint factory in Boundary Road, London. His exhibitions have always focused on contemporary artists and Saatchi's Sensation exhibition of Young British Artists in 1997 at the Royal Academy, London and at the Brooklyn Museum of Art, New York sparked an explosion of controversy.

Saatchi has been one of the moving forces of the modern age, vigorously shaping the contemporary art world, and was selected by the BBC as one of 60 'New Elizabethans' who have most influenced the past 60 years.

The 70,000 square foot Saatchi Gallery in the Duke of York's HQ King's Road is one of the largest showcases of contemporary art in the world. It has hosted fifteen of the twenty most visited exhibitions in London over the last 5 years in the Art Newspaper annual museum visitor surveys and is amongst the top five most popular museums in the world on Facebook, and Twitter, and Google+.

Saatchi's previous books include *Known Unknowns, Dead, The Naked Eye, Babble, Be The Worst You Can Be* and his first book *My Name Is Charles Saatchi and I'm an Artoholic* in which he answered questions from journalists, critics, and members of the public with brutally frank candour.